ENGLISH SPOKEN HERE

Consumer Information

Jerry L. Messec
Roger E. Kranich

CAMBRIDGE Adult Education
Prentice Hall Regents, Englewood Cliffs, NJ 07632

Executive Editor: Brian Schenk
Project Editor/Writer: Eva Holzer
Project Consultants: Laurel T. Ellis
Don Williams

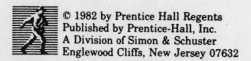 © 1982 by Prentice Hall Regents
Published by Prentice-Hall, Inc.
A Division of Simon & Schuster
Englewood Cliffs, New Jersey 07632

Printed in the United States of America

10 9 8 7 6 5 4 3 2

ISBN 0-8428-0851-5

Prentice-Hall International (UK) Limited, *London*
Prentice-Hall of Australia Pty. Limited, *Sydney*
Prentice-Hall Canada Inc., *Toronto*
Prentice-Hall Hispanoamericana, S.A., *Mexico*
Prentice-Hall of India Private Limited, *New Delhi*
Prentice-Hall of Japan, Inc., *Tokyo*
Simon & Schuster Asia Pte. Ltd., *Singapore*
Editora Prentice-Hall do Brasil, Ltda., *Rio de Janeiro*

CONTENTS

UNIT 1

HOW MUCH DOES IT COST?

IN THIS UNIT YOU WILL LEARN:

how to talk about money
how to ask for change
how to exchange money
how to ask about prices
how to say what you think about prices
how to compare money amounts
how to talk about mistakes in change

Notice these words and phrases in the unit:

How much is . . . ?
What's the price of . . . ?
How much does . . . cost?
is and **are** with money amounts
some, any
comparison words
one-dollar bill, five-dollar bill,
    ten-dollar bill, twenty-dollar bill
need, must have
questions with **which**

LOOK AT THE PICTURE.
Find these things in the picture.

1. washing machine (washer)
2. dryer
3. change machine
4. vending machines
5. attendant
6. clothes
7. counter
8. detergent
9. "out of order" sign
10. basket

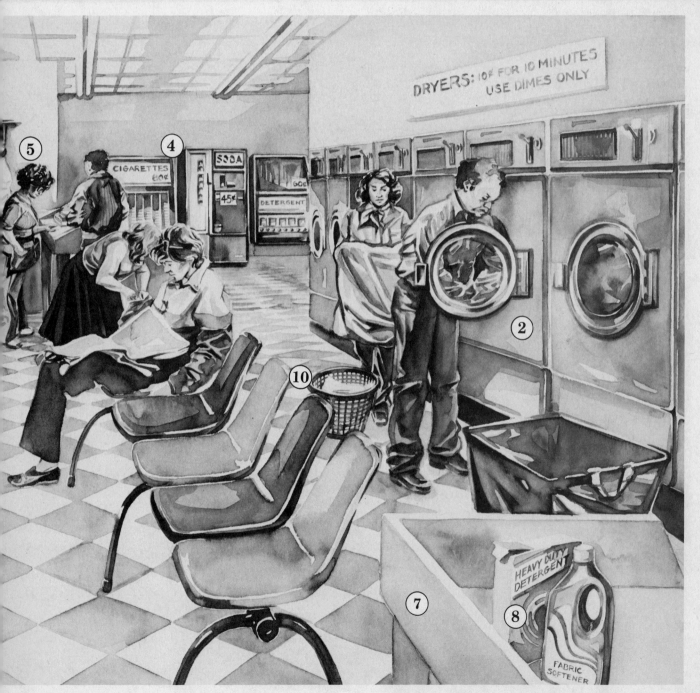

1

TALK TOPICS

LOOK AT THE PICTURES.
Talk about what you see.

Where are the people?
Where are the clothes?
What are the people doing?
What do the signs mean?

How much does it cost to use
a washing machine?
How many quarters do you need to use
one? How many quarters to use two?
What coins do you need for a dryer?
How many coins do you need to use a
dryer for 30 minutes?
What coins do you need to buy a soda?
cigarettes?

What are some differences between this
picture and the first one?
Who is the woman giving change
in the first picture?
Where was she in the first picture?
Where is she in this picture?

ASK ABOUT OTHER THINGS IN THE PICTURE.

Ask "What is this?" or "What do you call this?"
Write your new words.

11. _____ 16. _____
12. _____ 17. _____
13. _____ 18. _____
14. _____ 19. _____
15. _____ 20. _____

3

LOOK AT THESE PICTURES.
They show some of the money of the United States.

We use the words on the first line to say the names of the bills:
  This is a one-dollar bill.
We use the words on the second line to talk about amounts:
  I have one dollar.
  I need a buck.

a one-dollar bill
one dollar; a buck

a five-dollar bill
five dollars; five bucks

a ten-dollar bill
ten dollars; ten bucks

a twenty-dollar bill
twenty dollars; twenty bucks

We use the words on the first line to say the names of the coins:
  This is a penny.
We use the words on the second line to talk about amounts:
  I have one cent.

a penny
one cent

a nickel
five cents

a dime
ten cents

a quarter
twenty-five cents

4

LOOK AT THESE SYMBOLS.
They show how to write money amounts.

$$
\begin{array}{rcl}
\text{one cent} = & 1¢ = & \$.01 \\
\text{five cents} = & 5¢ = & \$.05 \\
\text{ten cents} = & 10¢ = & \$.10 \\
\text{twenty-five cents} = & 25¢ = & \$.25 \\
\text{fifty cents} = & 50¢ = & \$.50 \\
\text{one dollar} = & 100¢ = & \$1.00 \\
\text{five dollars} = & & \$5.00 \\
\text{ten dollars} = & & \$10.00 \\
\end{array}
$$

LOOK AT THESE PICTURES.
Write the symbols under each picture.

<u>   1¢   </u>   <u>   </u>   <u>   </u>   <u>   </u>

<u> \$.01 </u>   <u>   </u>   <u>   </u>   <u>   </u>

<u>   </u>   <u>   </u>

<u>   </u>   <u>   </u>

HOW MUCH MONEY?

Pennies

To count pennies, count by ones: one, two, three, four, five, six, seven, eight, nine, ten . . .

one penny = 1¢ ($.01)

three pennies = 3¢ ($.03)

five pennies = 5¢ ($.05)

Nickels

To count nickels, count by fives: five, ten, fifteen, twenty, twenty-five, thirty, thirty-five, forty, forty-five, fifty . . .

two nickels = 10¢ ($.10)

three nickels = 15¢ ($.15)

five nickels = 25¢ ($.25)

Dimes

To count dimes, count by tens: ten, twenty, thirty, forty, fifty, sixty, seventy, eighty, ninety, one dollar

three dimes = 30¢ ($.30)

five dimes = 50¢ ($.50)

ten dimes = 100¢ ($1.00)

Quarters

To count quarters, count by twenty-fives: twenty-five, fifty, seventy-five, one dollar

one quarter = 25¢ ($.25)

two quarters = 50¢ ($.50)

four quarters = $1.00

LOOK AT THESE COINS.
Count the money. Write the amount under each picture.

_____

_____

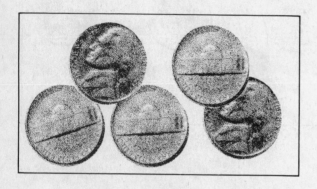

_____

_____

_____

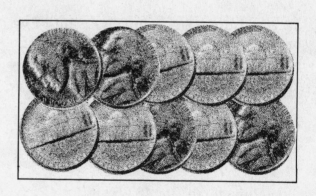

_____

_____

_____

_____

_____

_____

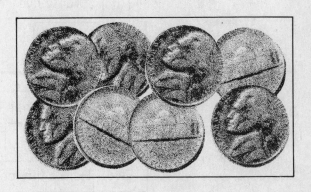

_____

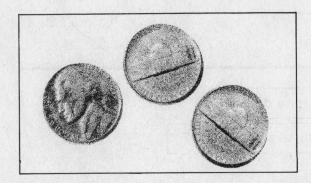

_____

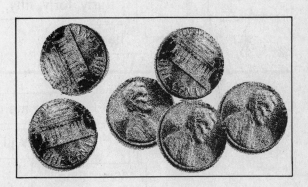

_____

HOW MANY?
Answer the questions.

A. How many pennies are there in a nickel? _____

B. How many pennies are there in a dime? _____

C. How many nickels are there in a dime? _____

D. How many nickels are there in a quarter? _____

E. How many dimes are there in a dollar? _____

F. How many quarters are there in a dollar? _____

MAKING CHANGE

LISTEN TO THESE PEOPLE.
They are asking for change.

Do you have change for a quarter?

I only have nickels. Is that all right?

That's fine.

Here you are. Five, ten, fifteen, twenty, twenty-five.

Thanks a lot.

I need some dimes for the dryer, please.

How many do you need?

Five. Here's fifty cents.

And here are your five dimes. Ten, twenty, thirty, forty, fifty.

Thanks.

Could you give me change for a dollar?

Will four quarters be all right?

Yes. Fine.

That's twenty-five, fifty, seventy-five, a dollar.

Thank you.

Can you change a five?

Sorry. I don't have any singles.

Thanks anyway.

Can I get change for a ten here?

Sorry. We don't give change. You have to buy something.

OK. I'll take a newspaper.

Here's your change and your paper.

Thanks.

FILL IN THE MISSING WORDS.
Ask for change.

A. Excuse _____ . Could you _____ me change for a quarter?

Will five _____ be all right?

That's _____ .

Here you _____ . Five, _____ , fifteen, _____ , twenty-five.

_____ .

B. Do you have change for a dollar?

I can give you _____ dimes.

_____ fine.

OK. Ten, twenty, _____ , _____ , fifty, sixty, _____ ,

_____ , _____ , a dollar.

_____ a lot.

C. I need some quarters _____ the parking meter.

How _____ do you need?

Four. Here's a _____ .

And here _____ four quarters. _____ , fifty, seventy-five,

_____ dollar.

_____ .

D. _____ you have any singles?

_____ many do you need?

Ten. Here's a ten-dollar _____ .

And here are your ten _____ .

_____ .

LISTEN TO THE BUS DRIVER.
He is talking about the fare.

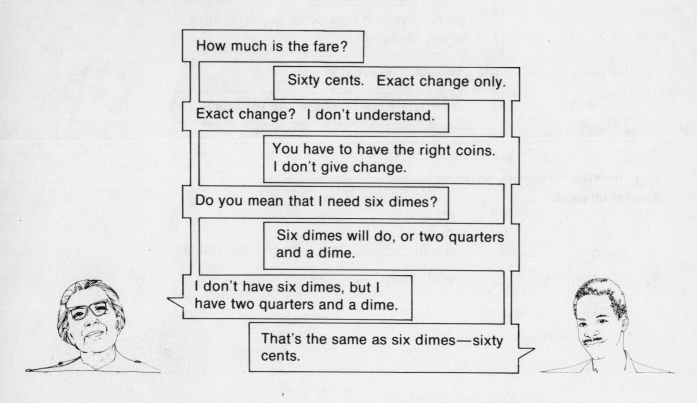

How much is the fare?

Sixty cents. Exact change only.

Exact change? I don't understand.

You have to have the right coins.
I don't give change.

Do you mean that I need six dimes?

Six dimes will do, or two quarters
and a dime.

I don't have six dimes, but I
have two quarters and a dime.

That's the same as six dimes—sixty
cents.

HOW MANY OF EACH COIN?
Show different coins that add up to 60¢.
Fill in the numbers.

A. _2_ quarters, _1_ dime

B. ___ dimes

C. ___ quarters, ___ nickels

D. ___ nickels

E. _1_ quarter, _3_ dimes, _1_ nickel

F. ___ quarter, ___ dimes, ___ nickels

G. ___ quarter, ___ dime, ___ nickels

H. ___ quarter, ___ nickels

TRY IT ON YOUR OWN.
Answer the questions.

A. What is the fare on the bus near your home? _____

B. Do you need exact change? _____

C. What coins can you use?

_____

_____

12

LOOK AT THESE PICTURES.
Count the money.
Write the amount under each picture.

_____

_____

_____

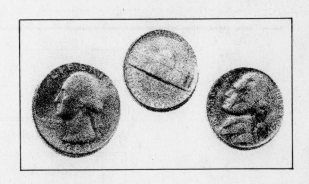

_____

_____

_____

_____

_____

13

LISTEN TO YOKO.
She is using a payphone.

Operator.

How much does it cost to call Philadelphia?

A dollar five for the first three minutes if you dial direct.

Dial direct? I don't understand.

If you dial the number yourself. Dial one, then the area code, and then the number you are calling. You don't need the operator.

Oh, I see. Thank you. I'll get some more change.

Please deposit a dollar five for the first three minutes.

Here are four quarters and a nickel.

Thank you.

Hello.

Hi, Sara. This is Yoko.

What a nice surprise! Where are you?

In Columbus. I can only talk for three minutes. I don't have any more change.

How much did this call cost?

A dollar five.

That's expensive!

It's not much. It's nice to hear your voice.

Well, next time, call in the evening. It costs less. Or call on the weekend.

TRY IT IN CLASS.
Write how many quarters, dimes, or nickels you need for the call.

A. That will be seventy cents for the first three minutes.

> 70¢ = 2 quarters and 2 dimes, or
>
> 70¢ = 2 quarters, a dime, and 2 nickels.

B. Please deposit ninety-five cents for the first three minutes.

95¢ = _____

C. Forty cents for the next three minutes, please.

40¢ = _____

D. Deposit a dollar thirty-five.

$1.35 = _____

E. One dollar seventy, please.

$1.70 = _____

F. That will be sixty-five cents for the first minute.

65¢ = _____

TRY IT IN CLASS.
Practice with another student.
One person is the operator.
The other person is the caller.
The operator tells how much the call is.
The caller tells what coins to deposit in the payphone.
Use these amounts: $2.05; $1.25; $1.85; $2.40.

OPERATOR: _____

CALLER: _____

ASKING ABOUT PRICES

LISTEN TO THESE PEOPLE.
They are talking about prices.

Excuse me. How much is this book?

Three ninety-five.

That's not much. I'll take it.

What's the cost of a call to Chicago?

Two fifteen for the first three minutes.

That's expensive.

It costs less if you dial direct.

How much is it then?

A dollar twenty-five.

That's a lot less. Thanks.

What's the price of a ticket?

Five dollars.

Oh, I don't have enough money.
I only have three dollars. I need two more.

These new cars are expensive.

How much do they cost?

About six thousand dollars.

That's a lot of money.

You can get a used car
for a thousand or two.

That's much cheaper.

FILL IN THE MISSING WORDS.
Talk about prices.

A. _____ much is this?

    Two fifty.

That's not _____ . I'll take _____ .

B. What's the _____ of a call to Boston?

    One ninety-five for the _____ three minutes.

_____ expensive.

    It costs _____ if you dial direct.

How _____ is it then?

    A dollar ten.

C. Taxis are expensive.

    How much does it _____ to go to your house?

About ten dollars.

    Wow! That's a _____ of money. How _____ the bus?

Fifty _____ per person.

    _____ much less. Let's take the bus.

D. Do you want to _____ to a movie?

    What's the _____ of a ticket?

Four fifty.

    I don't have _____ money.

How _____ do you have?

    Three fifty. I need one _____ dollar.

I'll give you a _____ . Let's go.

E. This restaurant _____ expensive.

Dinner _____ about twenty _____ .

    _____ a lot _____ money. How _____ the restaurant

on the corner?

You can _____ dinner there for five _____ six dollars.

    That's much _____ .

TALK TO THESE PEOPLE.
Tell them, "You have enough" or "You don't have enough."

A. I want to buy a soft drink for 70¢.
I have two quarters and a dime.
You _____

B. I want to call Los Angeles. The call costs $2.05.
I have three quarters and a nickel.
_____

C. I want to see a movie. The price of a ticket is $3.50.
I have a five-dollar bill.
_____

D. I want to have a hamburger and french fries.
A hamburger is 75¢ and french fries are 50¢.
I have four quarters, 3 dimes, and two nickels.
_____

E. I want to take the train to work. A ticket costs $1.50.
I have five quarters and three nickels.
_____

F. I need a book for school. It costs $2.95.
I have two dollar bills, four quarters, and three dimes.
_____

G. I want to buy a coat. It costs $55.00.
I have three ten-dollar bills, two five-dollar bills, and six one-dollar bills.
_____

H. I want to buy a new radio. It costs $85.00.
I have six ten-dollar bills and seven five-dollar bills.
_____

I. I need an umbrella. There are umbrellas for sale on the corner for $3.98.
I have 3 dollar bills, 2 quarters, and 2 nickels.
_____

J. I want to buy a new record. It costs $6.98.
I have a five-dollar bill, two one-dollar bills, and 3 quarters.
_____

18

LOOK AT THE SIGNS.
Write a sentence about each sign. Use <u>must have</u> or <u>need</u>.
Talk about what the signs mean.

A.

FARE 60¢
Exact change required

You need exact change. **OR**

You must have exact change. **OR**

You must have 60 cents in change.

B.

Dryers
10¢ for 10 min.
Dimes Only

_____

_____

C.

Toll $1.00
Exact Change Lane

_____

_____

D.

TOKENS ONLY

_____

_____

E.

All Day Parking 50¢
QUARTERS ONLY

_____

_____

Where do you find these signs?

What other things do you need exact change for?

COMPARING PRICES

LISTEN TO THESE PEOPLE.
They are comparing prices.

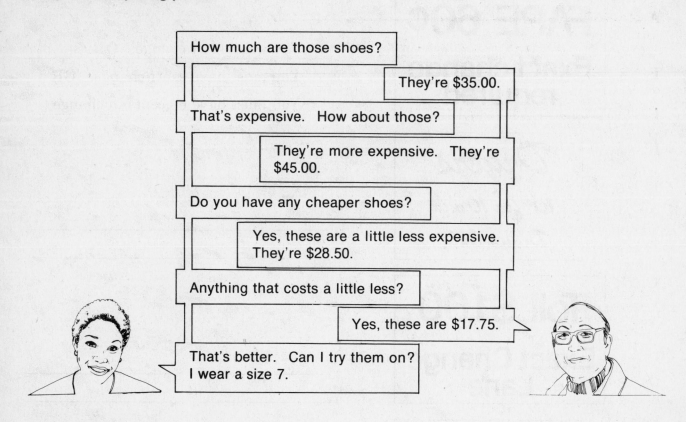

How much are those shoes?

They're $35.00.

That's expensive. How about those?

They're more expensive. They're $45.00.

Do you have any cheaper shoes?

Yes, these are a little less expensive. They're $28.50.

Anything that costs a little less?

Yes, these are $17.75.

That's better. Can I try them on? I wear a size 7.

TRY IT IN CLASS.
Compare these prices.
Mark the right answer.

$5.95

$28.00

$12.00

$8.95

A.	Which is more expensive?	the shirt	the pants
B.	Which is cheaper?	the hat	the gloves
C.	Which costs less?	the hat	the shirt
D.	Which costs more?	the pants	the gloves
E.	Which is less expensive?	the shirt	the gloves

FILL IN THE MISSING WORDS.
Practice comparing prices.
Use these words: more expensive, less expensive,
                   cheaper, costs less, costs more

A.   A shirt that costs $5.95 is _____ than a shirt that costs
$9.95.

B.   A $25.00 dress is _____ than a $20.00 dress.

C.   A $65.00 coat is _____ than a $600.00 coat.

D.   A car for $900.00 _____ than a car for $5,000.00.

E.   A color TV for $375.00 _____ than a black-and-white TV for
$89.00.

F.   A taxi ride for $10.00 is _____ than a bus ride for $.75.

G.   A book for $25.00 _____ than a book for $15.50.

H.   A steak that costs $3.95 per pound is _____ than hamburger
that costs $1.89 per pound.

TRY IT IN CLASS.
Practice with another student.
Compare the prices.

A.   A trip that costs $175.00 and a trip that costs $250.00.

_____

B.   Lunch for $12.50 and lunch for $3.99.

_____

C.   A hotel room for $23.00 and a hotel room for $58.00.

_____

D.   A phone call in the daytime for $1.25 for three minutes, and a
phone call at night for $.50 for three minutes.

_____

E.   A color TV that costs $350.00 and a black-and-white TV that costs
$89.00.

_____

MISTAKES IN CHANGE

LISTEN TO THESE PEOPLE.
They are talking about mistakes in change.

I think you gave me the wrong change. I gave you a ten-dollar bill, but you gave me change for a five.

Oh, I'm sorry. Here's five more.

That's all right.

Excuse me. I think you gave me too much change.

Did I?

Yes. You gave me a dollar too much.

Thank you for telling me.

Excuse me. You owe me another quarter.

Do I?

Yes. The change should be seventy-five cents.

You're right. I'm sorry. Here you are.

That's OK.

Did you make a mistake in the change you gave me?

What did I give you?

Two nickels instead of two quarters.

Sorry.

No problem.

Don't you owe me another dollar?

I don't think so. Didn't I give you three singles?

Oh yes. You did. Sorry. I didn't see the third one.

That's all right.

FILL IN THE MISSING WORDS.
Talk about mistakes in change.

A. I _____ you gave me the wrong _____ .

Did _____ ?

Yes. I gave you a five-dollar _____ but you

gave me change _____ one.

I'm _____ . Here are four _____ .

That's all _____ .

B. Did you make a _____ in the change you _____ me?

What did I _____ you?

A dollar _____ of ten dollars.

_____ .

That's _____ right.

C. I think you gave me _____ much change.

_____ I?

Yes. You gave me a dime too _____ .

Thank you for _____ me.

TRY IT IN CLASS.
Practice with another student.

You are a customer. Tell the sales clerk about a mistake in the change.

CUSTOMER: _____

SALES CLERK: _____

LOOK AT THIS BILL.
It is for some books.

CLAUDE'S BOOK STORE

DATE _7/1/82_

Gone With the Wind	$2⁹⁵
The Joy of Cooking	3²⁵
Webster's Dictionary	1⁵⁰
	7⁷⁰
TAX	.62
TOTAL	$8.32

NOW, LOOK AT THIS CHECK.
It is for the books on the bill.

LIN LEE   NO. __180__

                                                        1-21/201
                                    July 1 19 _82_

PAY TO THE
ORDER OF _Claude's Book Store_ _____ $ _8.32_

Eight and ³²/₁₀₀ _____ DOLLARS

PEOPLE'S BANK

1632 State St.
Shoreview, N.J. 08722

                        Lin Lee

:023000326:   026:::2382225

Look at the bills. Are they correct?
Write the checks.

JULIE'S CLOTHING

DATE _9-23-82_

1 SHIRT	$12.95
1 PR. SLACKS	25.00
	37.95
TAX	3.04
TOTAL	$40.99

CARMEN PEREZ	NO. **201**
	Sept. 23 19 _82_
PAY TO THE ORDER OF _Julie's Clothing_	$ _____
Forty and 99/100	
BANK OF THE CITY	_Carmen Perez_

FAMILY DEPARTMENT STOR'

DATE _8/18/82_

1 sheet	$8.75
1 blanket	20.00
2 pillows	17.50
	46.50
TAX	3.25
TOTAL	$49.95

GEORGE TERZA	NO. **145**
	Aug. 18 19 _82_
PAY TO THE ORDER OF _Family Department Store_	$ _____
FIRST BANK	_George Terza_

ALPHA APPLIANCES

DATE _7-23-82_

TC Color TV mod. 28B2	$259⁹⁵
TAX	20⁸⁰
TOTAL	$279⁷⁵

TERESA BROWN	NO. **215**
	_____ 19 ___
PAY TO THE ORDER OF _Alpha Appliances_	$ _____
PEOPLE'S BANK	_____

CLOSE-UP ON LANGUAGE

Using some and any in questions and answers

In questions, use either some or any:

Do you have any change?   Do you have some change?
Is there any detergent in the box?   Is there some detergent in the box?
Are there any less expensive ones?   Are there some less expensive ones?

In answers, use some with "yes" (positive answers), and
               use any with "no" (negative answers):

No, there isn't any detergent.   Yes, there is some detergent.
I don't have any change.   I have some change.
There aren't any.   There are some.

FILL IN THE MISSING WORDS.
Use some or any.

A.   Are there ___any___ people in the store?

B.   I don't have _____ quarters.

C.   He has _____ change to give you.

D.   Do you need _____ dimes for the dryer?

E.   There isn't _____ milk for the coffee.

F.   Is there _____ time left?

G.   There are _____ cookies on the table.

H.   Would you like _____ food?

I.   There aren't _____ books in the classroom.

J.   They have _____ work to do.

K.   Can you give me _____ cold water?

L.   There is _____ ice cream in the freezer.

M.   We don't need _____ more.

N.   I can't find _____ cheaper ones.

O.   Did you see _____ cars?

Using is and are with money amounts

Money amounts and words for things you can't count take a singular verb.
Use is:

Here is ten dollars.   That is $14.25.
This is 25¢.   Here is some change.
Is there any money left?   How much is the salary?

Coins or bills (like words for things you can count) take a plural verb.
Use are:

Here are five one-dollar bills.
Here are ten dimes.
There are four quarters in a dollar.
Are there any singles in the drawer?
There are some pennies in the box.

FILL IN THE MISSING WORDS.
Use is or are.

A.   Here _____ two nickels.

B.   Here _____ ten cents.

C.   There _____ $100.00 in the cash register.

D.   There _____ three five-dollar bills on the table.

E.   These _____ pennies.

F.   This _____ five dollars.

G.   This _____ a five-dollar bill.

H.   A quarter _____ a twenty-five cent coin.

I.   _____ there any change in the cash register?

J.   There _____ some money on the table.

K.   There _____ no money left in my bank account.

L.   There _____ no quarters left in the drawer.

M.   _____ there enough time to have some coffee?

N.   _____ there any cookies left?

O.   How many dimes _____ there in the box?

P.   Here _____ the money you asked for.

Words for comparing two things

Add er to one-syllable words:

cheap	.....cheaper		new	..... newer
big	..... bigger		old	.....older
small	.....smaller		tall	..... taller

Add er to words that end with y (change the y to i):

happy	..... happier		funny	.....funnier
pretty	..... prettier		heavy	.....heavier

Use more with words that have more than two syllables:

expensive	.....more expensive		delicious	.....more delicious
intelligent	.....more intelligent		interesting	.....more interesting

FILL IN THE MISSING WORDS.
Practice making comparisons.

A. The bus is _____ than a taxi.   (cheap)

B. The theater is _____ than the movies.   (expensive)

C. He is _____ than I am.   (rich)

D. Miami is _____ than New York.   (warm)

E. He is _____ than his brother.   (young)

F. This room is _____ than the other one.   (sunny)

G. My boss is _____ than I am.   (experienced)

H. This book is _____ than that one.   (difficult)

 I. I am _____ now than I was an hour ago.   (hungry)

J. This chair is _____ than that one.   (comfortable)

K. Do you have a _____ jacket to wear?   (light)

L. The _____ one is nicer.   (small)

M. This is a picture of my _____ sister.   (old)

N. It would be _____ to meet in front of the theater.   (easy)

O. I think this program is _____ than that one.   (interesting)

Questions with <u>which</u>

Notice how <u>which</u> is used in these questions:

Comparisons	Choices
<u>Which</u> book is more expensive?	<u>Which</u> one do you want?
<u>Which</u> way is shorter?	<u>Which</u> one is the teacher?
<u>Which</u> dress is prettier?	<u>Which</u> is your coat?

Use <u>which</u> when you refer to specific things:
    <u>Which</u> do you like better, coffee or tea?
Use <u>what</u> when you refer to things in general:
    <u>What</u> do you like to drink?

FILL IN THE MISSING WORDS.
Use one of these question words: <u>who</u>, <u>what</u>, <u>where</u>, <u>which</u>.
(See "English Spoken Here: Getting Started" to review <u>who</u>, <u>what</u>, and <u>where</u>.)

A. _____ did you put your coat?

B. _____ told you about the job?

C. _____ one of these offices is Mr. Young in?

D. _____ one of these applications is yours?

E. _____ kind of job are you looking for?

F. _____ way is the post office?

G. _____ can I find an elevator?

H. _____ is the next person in line?

 I. _____ is the cheaper of the two?

J. _____ of these two buildings is taller?

K. _____ is the price of this chair?

L. _____ of the two chairs is more comfortable?

M. _____ is paying the bill?

N. _____ of these two newspapers did you read?

O. _____ did you say?

P. _____ one of these doors should I open?

Q. _____ did you come from?

R. _____ restaurant are we going to, Mario's or Frank's?

S. _____ is the name of that man?

T. _____ did you get that pretty blouse?

PRACTICE ON YOUR OWN

A. Ask a friend for change for: a quarter,
a dollar, a five-dollar bill.

B. Look at this chart or the chart in your local phone book.

Dial direct	Weekday full rate 8 A.M. to 5 P.M.	
Sample rates to:	First minute	Each additional minute
Atlanta, Ga.	.53	.36
Atlantic City, N.J.	.45	.30
Boston, Mass.	.46	.32
Chicago, Ill.	.53	.36
Denver, Colo.	.55	.38
Detroit, Mich.	.53	.36
Houston, Tex.	.55	.38
Miami, Fla.	.55	.38
New Orleans, La.	.55	.38
Philadelphia, Pa.	.45	.30
Seattle, Wash.	.57	.40
Washington, D.C.	.48	.34

(1) Get the right change ready for a one-minute call to
Atlantic City.

_____

(2) Get the right change ready for a one-minute call to Houston.

_____

(3) Get the right change ready for a two-minute call to
Philadelphia.

_____

(4) Get the right change ready for a three-minute call to
Washington, D.C.

_____

(5) Get the right change ready for a three-minute call to Boston.

_____

(6) Get the right change ready for a three-minute call to Detroit.

_____

C. Practice with another person.
Compare the prices of some phone calls.
Ask questions like these:

(1) Which is cheaper, a one-minute call to Atlantic City or a one-minute call to Houston?

(2) Which is more expensive, a three-minute call to Washington, D.C., or a three-minute call to Boston?

D. Find out what the bus fare is on a bus near your home. Get exact change ready for the bus.

E. Go to some stores. Write down the prices of some TV's, radios, cameras, clothes, toys and jewelry. Compare the prices. Tell a friend about them.

F. Count the change you get after buying something. If you get the wrong change, tell the sales clerk or cashier.

UNIT 2

WHICH STORE HAS THE BEST PRICES?

IN THIS UNIT YOU WILL LEARN:

how to talk about food (food names)
how to ask what another person
    wants to buy
how to read food ads and store coupons
how to ask where things are in a
    supermarket
how to talk about food quantities
    and sizes of packages
how to compare products
how to make suggestions
how to understand unit pricing

Notice these words and phrases in the unit:

else (What else? Anything else?)
kind (What kind? Which kind?)
better, worse
best, worst, and other superlatives
bought, paid, ate, drank, and a
    review of other irregular past
    tense words
let's, could, how about, and
    why don't for making suggestions
imperatives (words telling
    someone to do something)
above, below, under, next to,
    in front of, in back of, on top of,
    to the left of, and **to the right of**

32

LOOK AT THE PICTURE.
Find these words in the picture.

1. aisle
2. check-out counter
3. cash register
4. shelves
5. shopping cart
6. aisle numbers
7. express check-out
8. check-cashing counter
9. sale announcement
10. scale

TALK TOPICS

LOOK AT THE PICTURES.
Talk about what you see.

What is this place?
What is an express check-out?
What are some of the things people
    can buy here?
What is a check-cashing counter?
How can you get a check-cashing card?

Which of the products do you buy?
Which are not familiar to you?
What is the scale for?
How can you make sure you were charged
    the right amount of money?

What are some differences between this
    picture and the first one?
Talk about what has changed.

ASK ABOUT OTHER THINGS IN THE PICTURE.
Use all of these question words: who, what, where, which, how.
Write your new words.

11. _____   16. _____

12. _____   17. _____

13. _____   18. _____

14. _____   19. _____

15. _____   20. _____

GOING SHOPPING

LISTEN TO THESE PEOPLE.
They are talking about shopping.

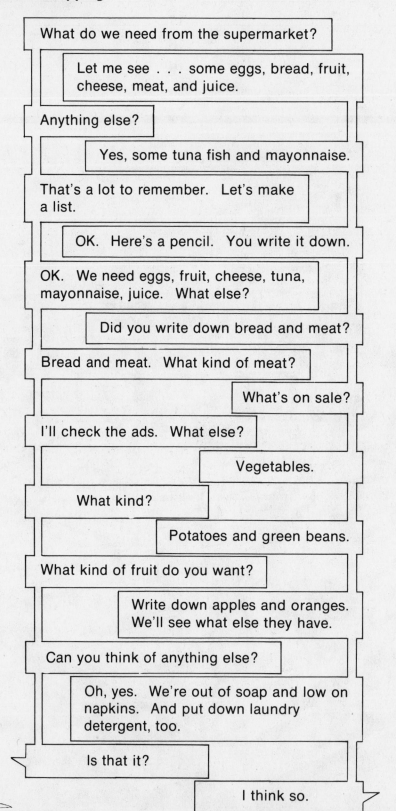

What do we need from the supermarket?

Let me see . . . some eggs, bread, fruit, cheese, meat, and juice.

Anything else?

Yes, some tuna fish and mayonnaise.

That's a lot to remember. Let's make a list.

OK. Here's a pencil. You write it down.

OK. We need eggs, fruit, cheese, tuna, mayonnaise, juice. What else?

Did you write down bread and meat?

Bread and meat. What kind of meat?

What's on sale?

I'll check the ads. What else?

Vegetables.

What kind?

Potatoes and green beans.

What kind of fruit do you want?

Write down apples and oranges. We'll see what else they have.

Can you think of anything else?

Oh, yes. We're out of soap and low on napkins. And put down laundry detergent, too.

Is that it?

I think so.

36

FILL IN THE MISSING WORDS.
Practice talking about shopping.

TOM: What do we _____ from the grocery store?

MARY: We need _____ potatoes, cereal, juice, and fruit.

TOM: Anything _____ ?

MARY: Yes. We need _____ cheese.

TOM: What kind _____ cheese?

MARY: Let's _____ some cheddar.

TOM: And what _____ of fruit _____ you want?

MARY: We'll _____ some pears and grapes. We'll _____ what _____ they have at the store.

TOM: Can you _____ of anything else?

MARY: Oh _____ . We're _____ of coffee, and low _____ sugar.

TOM: _____ else?

MARY: No, that's _____ .

TALK TO THIS PERSON.
This person is answering your questions. Ask the questions.

YOU: _____
PERSON: We need some fruit, meat, and cheese.

YOU: _____
PERSON: Yes. We need some vegetables.

YOU: _____
PERSON: Let's get some broccoli, carrots, and spinach.

YOU: _____
PERSON: How about cheddar cheese and Swiss cheese?

YOU: _____
PERSON: Get apples, pears, and oranges.

YOU: _____
PERSON: We could buy hamburger and pork chops.

YOU: _____
PERSON: No. That's it.

LOOK AT THESE PICTURES.
They show some of the things that
Mary and Peter need from the store.
Write what each picture shows.
Use Peter's shopping list.

eggs
fruit — apples, oranges, bananas
cheese
milk
bread
meat — hamburger, chicken
vegetables — potatoes, carrots
soap
napkins   detergent
juice   tuna

_____

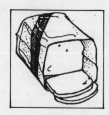
_____

_____

_____

_____

_____

_____

_____

_____

_____

_____

_____

_____

_____

_____

_____

TRY IT ON YOUR OWN.
Practice making a shopping list.

What do you buy every week?
What do you have in the house?
What do you need?

Write what you need on the list.

```
┌─────────────────────────────────────┐
│           SHOPPING LIST             │
│  _____  │
│  _____  │
│  _____  │
│  _____  │
│  _____  │
│  _____  │
└─────────────────────────────────────┘
```

FILL IN THIS SHOPPING LIST.
You have $25.00.
You are shopping at Milk Barn.
What will you buy?
Use the price list on the right.

SHOPPING LIST

Food	Price
_____	$.
_____	.
_____	.
_____	.
_____	.
_____	.
_____	.
_____	.
TOTAL $	.

MILK BARN PRICE LIST

Food	Price
Bread....................................	$ .99 a loaf
Milk.......................................	$ .65 a quart
Eggs......................................	$1.09 a dozen
Cheese..................................	$2.89 a pound
Tuna......................................	$ .89 a can
Chicken.................................	$ .79 a pound
Lettuce..................................	$ .69 a head
Tomatoes..............................	$ .75 a pound
Carrots..................................	$ .55 a bunch
Butter....................................	$1.01 a pound
Green Beans........................	$1.00 for 3 cans
Oranges................................	$1.00 for 6
Strawberries........................	$ .89 a box

Which store do you want to go to?

Let's look at the ads in the newspaper.

What for?

They advertise sales. We'll see which store has the best prices this week.

You mean they don't all have the same prices. How come?

Stores have special sales to get people to shop there.

Really?

Look at these ads for orange juice. It costs $1.09 in one and $1.29 in another.

Look. This store has lamb chops on sale. Is $2.29 a pound a good price?

That's less than the price I paid last week.

Then let's go there.

OK. How much money do you have?

I have $35.00. Is that enough?

Well, I have about $30.00. I'm sure $65.00 should be enough.

TALK TO THIS PERSON.
Practice asking for more information. Use "What for?" "How come?" and "Really?"

PERSON: I buy the newspaper every Wednesday.
YOU: _____

PERSON: I always look at the ads.
YOU: _____

PERSON: I find out which store has the cheapest prices.
YOU: _____

40

LOOK AT THESE FOOD ADS.
Answer the questions.

U.S.D.A. GRADE "A" **Fresh Young Turkeys** **67¢** 10 to 14 lb. 18 to 22 lb. Average lb.	100% Pure Florida Orange Juice **Premium Pack Tropicala** **1²⁹** half gal. cont.	U.S.D.A. Choice Fresh American Grown Lamb (Shoulder) **Lamb Chops** **2²⁹** lb.
		Western **Fresh Broccoli** Large Bunch **79¢** ea.
		Large 88 Size California **Navel Oranges** **7** for **$1**
Large Size Firm Ripe **Slicing Tomatoes** **49¢** lb.	Limit 4 With Each Additional $7.50 Purchase **Buzz Bee** **Chunk Light Tuna** **69¢** 6½ oz. can Tuna In Oil or Water As Avail.	**Red Delicious Apples** **49¢** lb. U.S. #1 2½" min.
		U.S.D.A. GRADE "A" Broiling or Frying **Chickens** **55¢** lb. Whole Up to 3 lbs. (Quartered or Split lb. 59¢)

A. How many oranges can you get for $1.00?

_____

B. How much does 2 pounds of lamb chops cost?

_____

C. How much tuna fish do you get for 69¢?

_____

D. How much is a half-gallon of orange juice?

_____

E. How much is two pounds of chicken that is quartered?

_____

F. How much broccoli can you get for 79¢?

_____

G. How many cans of tuna fish can you get if you don't buy anything else?

_____

LOOK AT THESE COUPONS.
They can only be used at one supermarket.
Answer the questions.

WALLBROWN'S	WALLBROWN'S	WALLBROWN'S	WALLBROWN'S
Green Dish Liquid	Royal Stick Margarine	100 Upton Tea Bags	Tried Detergent
1 49 quart cont. Limit 4 conts. with coupon.	**59¢** 1 lb. pkg. Limit 4 pkgs. with coupon	**1** 57 pkg. Limit 4 pkgs. with coupon	**2** 99 5 lb. 4 oz. box Limit 4 boxes with coupon
limit 1 coupon per shopping family good til Sat. night, Jan. 15, 1983	limit 1 coupon per shopping family good til Sat. night, Jan. 15, 1983	limit 1 coupon per shopping family good til Sat. night, Jan. 15, 1983	limit 1 coupon per shopping family good til Sat. night, Jan. 15, 1983
WALLBROWN'S	WALLBROWN'S	WALLBROWN'S	WALLBROWN'S
Snow Spray Oven Cleaner	Fabric Softener Half Gallon Last Touch	Sticks 8 oz. or Slices 10 oz. Diet Day Cheese Food	This Coupon Worth **50¢** Towards the Purchase of Any 1 lb. 12 oz. jar Lumpy Peanut Butter
1 09 pint can Limit 4 cans with coupon	**1** 79 cont. Limit 4 conts. with coupon.	**1** 39 pkg. Limit 4 pkgs. with coupon	Limit 4 jars with coupon
limit 1 coupon per shopping family good til Sat. night, Jan. 15, 1983	limit 1 coupon per shopping family good til Sat. night, Jan. 15, 1983	limit 1 coupon per shopping family good til Sat. night, Jan. 15, 1983	limit 1 coupon per shopping family good til Sat. night, Jan. 15, 1983

A. Where can you use these coupons?

_____

B. What is the last day you can use these coupons?

_____

C. What size box of detergent can you buy with the coupon?

_____

D. How many pounds of margarine can you buy with the coupon?

_____

E. Which is a better buy: cheese food in slices or in a stick?

_____

F. What brand of peanut butter can you get for 50¢ savings?

_____

G. How many packages of tea bags can you buy with the coupon?

_____

LOOK AT THESE COUPONS.
They can be used in any store.
They are called manufacturer's coupons.
Answer the questions.

A. Does the toothpaste coupon tell you what size you must buy?

_____

B. Does the toilet paper coupon tell you how many rolls you
must buy?

_____

C. How many bars of soap must you buy to save 15¢?

_____

D. Can you use the coffee coupon to save 40¢ on a can of
regular coffee?

_____

E. Can you save 20¢ on one roll of paper towels?

_____

QUANTITIES

LISTEN TO THESE PEOPLE.
They are talking about quantities and sizes.

Is a dozen eggs enough?

No. I think we need two dozen.

How about the cheese? How much do we need?

Get a small package of Swiss.

Anything else from the dairy section? Butter or milk?

We don't need butter, but we need a quart of milk.

What about orange juice? This brand is on sale for $1.09 a half gallon.

That's a good price. It's much better than the price I usually pay.

OK. Where's the meat section?

I think it's at the back of the store.

There it is. How much hamburger do we need?

About a pound and a half.

And how many packages of lamb chops?

How many chops in a package?

Four or five.

Then get two packages. Do you think this chicken is big enough?

How much does it weigh?

Three pounds and ten ounces. It's the biggest one here.

Yes, it's big enough.

44

TALK TO THESE PEOPLE.
Tell them what you need from the supermarket.
Use these quantity and size words: dozen, package, pound,
quart, can, head, bunch, bag, jar, box, loaf.

A. I need a _____ quart of milk _____ . (milk)

B. Please get a _____ . (lettuce)

C. Could you get a 5-pound _____ ? (potatoes)

D. We could use a _____ . (carrots)

E. _____ . (soup)

F. _____ . (apples)

G. _____ . (eggs)

H. _____ . (broccoli)

I. _____ . (cereal)

J. _____ . (bread)

K. _____ . (rolls)

L. _____ . (mayonnaise)

M. _____ . (butter)

N. _____ . (cabbage)

LOOK AT THESE ABBREVIATIONS.
Match the abbreviations with the words.

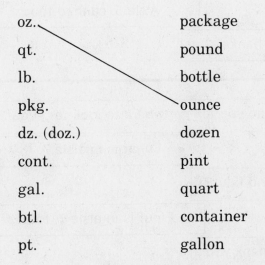

oz.	package
qt.	pound
lb.	bottle
pkg.	ounce
dz. (doz.)	dozen
cont.	pint
gal.	quart
btl.	container
pt.	gallon

LISTEN TO THESE PEOPLE.
They are asking for directions in the supermarket.

Where can I find detergent?

Aisle 6, cleaning products.

Thank you.

What aisle are the napkins in?

Aisle 3, paper products.

Thanks.

Excuse me. I'm looking for corn flakes.

That's in aisle 4 with the cereals.

Aisle 4? Thanks a lot.

Where can I find mayonnaise?

Mayonnaise is in aisle 2 next to the oil.

And tuna fish?

Aisle 5, canned food.

Thanks.

Can you tell me where to look for sugar?

Sugar is in aisle 7.

And flour?

Flour is in aisle 7, too.

Thank you.

LOOK AT THESE SECTION HEADINGS.
They show what is in each part of the supermarket.
Write the words from the shopping list under the right headings.

DAIRY PRODUCTS
milk
_____
_____

MEATS
_____
_____
_____

FROZEN FOOD
_____
_____
_____

BAKED GOODS
_____
_____

PRODUCE
_____
_____

PAPER PRODUCTS
_____
_____

DRUGS & COSMETICS
_____
_____
_____

CLEANING PRODUCTS
_____
_____
_____

CANNED FOODS
_____
_____
_____

CRACKERS & COOKIES
_____
_____
_____

JAMS, JELLIES
_____
_____
_____

OIL, SALAD DRESSINGS
_____
_____
_____

MACARONI PRODUCTS
(PASTA) & RICE
_____
_____
_____

CEREALS &
BREAKFAST DRINKS
_____
_____
_____

SODA
_____
_____
_____

SHOPPING LIST

milk	butter	Italian dressing	corn flakes
chicken	ice cream	spaghetti	brown rice
bananas	onions	napkins	ginger ale
shampoo	bread	oatmeal	potatoes
steak	grape jelly	toothpaste	paper towels
tuna	floor wax	furniture polish	graham crackers
muffins	TV dinner	cottage cheese	olive oil
toilet paper	bologna	canned tomatoes	bleach
oatmeal cookies	frozen pizza	cupcakes	club soda

47

LOOK AT THIS SUPERMARKET SECTION.
It is where the baking needs are.

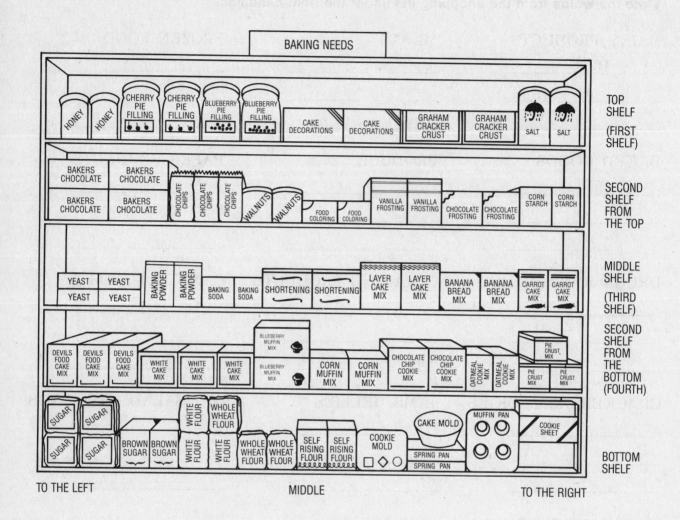

FILL IN THE MISSING WORDS.

A. The cake decorations are on the _____ shelf.

B. The sugar is on the _____ shelf.

C. The pie crust mix is on the _____ shelf.

D. The yeast is on the _____ shelf.

E. The flour is in the _____ of the bottom shelf.

F. The white cake mix is to the _____ of the devil's food cake mix.

G. The carrot cake mix is to the _____ of the banana bread mix.

H. The walnuts are in the _____ of the second shelf from the top.

I. The blueberry muffin mix is _____ the whole wheat flour.   (above, below)

J. The graham cracker crust is _____ the frosting.   (above, below)

48

TALK TO THESE PEOPLE.
Tell them where to find what they are looking for.
Look at the baking needs section on page 48.

A. PERSON: Where can I find layer cake mix?

YOU: _____On the middle shelf, to the right of the shortening._____

B. PERSON: Where can I find baker's chocolate?

YOU: _____

C. PERSON: Can you tell me where the self-rising flour is?

YOU: _____

D. PERSON: Where is the oatmeal cookie mix?

YOU: _____

E. PERSON: Can you tell me where I can find baking powder?

YOU: _____

F. PERSON: Where can I find some brown sugar?

YOU: _____

G. PERSON: Do you know where the vanilla frosting is?

YOU: _____

H. PERSON: I am trying to find a muffin pan.

YOU: _____

I. PERSON: Can you tell me where the chocolate chips are?

YOU: _____

J. PERSON: I am looking for the honey. Do you know where it is?

YOU: _____

K. PERSON: Do you know where the corn muffin mix is?

YOU: _____

L. PERSON: I'm looking for some cherry pie filling. Can you help me find it?

YOU: _____

COMPARING PRODUCTS

LISTEN TO THESE PEOPLE.
They are comparing products at the store.

Which brand of tuna do you want, Star Light or Buzz Bee?

Get Buzz Bee. It's better than Star Light.

Don't you like Star Light any more?

It's good, but I think Buzz Bee is better.

Is this brand of coffee OK?

No. That brand is terrible. I bought it once and couldn't drink it.

How about this one?

That one is even worse. It's the worst coffee I ever drank.

How about this brand?

That one's not bad. I liked it.

Let's get it, then.

Which ketchup do you want me to get?

Get Hern's. It's the best.

What size?

Get the largest bottle. We use a lot of ketchup.

Which kind of napkins do you want? There are so many.

I don't care. Get the cheapest.

FILL IN THE MISSING WORDS.
Practice comparing products.

A. _____ brand of orange juice do you want, the store brand _____ Sunshine?

Which is _____ ?

The store _____ is 83¢ a quart, and Sunshine is 99¢.

Then get the _____ _____ . It's _____ .

B. Which brand _____ detergent do you _____ ? Pride or Shore?

_____ Pride. It's _____ than Shore.

Don't you like Shore _____ more?

It's _____ , _____ I think Pride is _____ .

C. Is this _____ of paper towels OK?

_____ , that brand is _____ . I _____ it once and couldn't do

much with it.

How _____ this one?

That one is even _____ . It's the _____ paper towel I ever used.

And _____ brand?

That one's not _____ . I liked it.

_____ buy it, _____ .

D. _____ mayonnaise _____ you want me _____ get?

Get Heavenly. It's the _____ .

What _____ ?

Get the _____ jar. We use a lot _____ mayonnaise.

E. Should I get this _____ of ice cream? It's _____ cheapest.

It may be the _____ , but it's also the worst. I think

Taste Test is much _____ .

Let's _____ Parson's. It's the _____ delicious ice cream

I ever tasted.

Really? It may be the most _____ , and it's also

the _____ expensive ice cream I ever bought.

TRY IT IN CLASS.
Practice with another student.
Compare these products.
Use these words: biggest, cheapest, most expensive

| Mazel Corn Oil $2.29 48-oz. btl. | Caro Corn Oil $1.59 48-oz. btl. | Criscope Corn Oil $2.59 64-oz. btl. |

A. _____

B. _____

C. _____

TRY IT ON YOUR OWN.
Use these words: better, worse, sweeter, more delicious, softer,
**   best, worst, sweetest, most delicious, softest**

A.   Compare two brands of toothpaste.

_____

B.   Compare two brands of laundry detergent.

_____

C.   Compare two brands of ice cream.

_____

D.   Compare three brands of soft drink (soda).

_____

E.   Compare three brands of tuna fish.

_____

F.   Compare three brands of paper towels.

_____

G.   Compare three types of cheese.

_____

UNIT PRICING

To compare two products of different sizes, find the unit price label
on the shelf:

ITEM PRICE	UNIT PRICE
$2.29	4.77¢ per oz.
MAZEL CORN OIL 48-oz.	

ITEM PRICE	UNIT PRICE
$2.89	4.51¢ per oz.
MAZEL CORN OIL 64-oz.	

The unit price of the 64-oz. bottle is less than the unit price of
the 48-oz. bottle. The 64-oz. bottle is a better buy.

LOOK AT THE UNIT PRICE LABELS.
Which one is a better buy?

ITEM PRICE	UNIT PRICE
$1.39	17.3¢ per oz.
DEFEND TOOTHPASTE 8-oz.	

ITEM PRICE	UNIT PRICE
$.99	19.8¢ per oz.
DEFEND TOOTHPASTE 5-oz.	

The _____-oz. tube of toothpaste is the better buy.

ITEM PRICE	UNIT PRICE
$.85	53¢ per 100
HOUSTON NAPKINS 160 ct.	

ITEM PRICE	UNIT PRICE
$1.62	54¢ per 100
HOUSTON NAPKINS 300 ct.	

The _____ package of napkins is _____ .

ITEM PRICE	UNIT PRICE
$.99	33¢ per lb.
UNCLE SAM'S RICE 3 lb.	

ITEM PRICE	UNIT PRICE
$2.29	22.9¢ per lb.
UNCLE SAM'S RICE 10 lb.	

LISTEN TO THESE PEOPLE.
They are talking about the check-out counter.

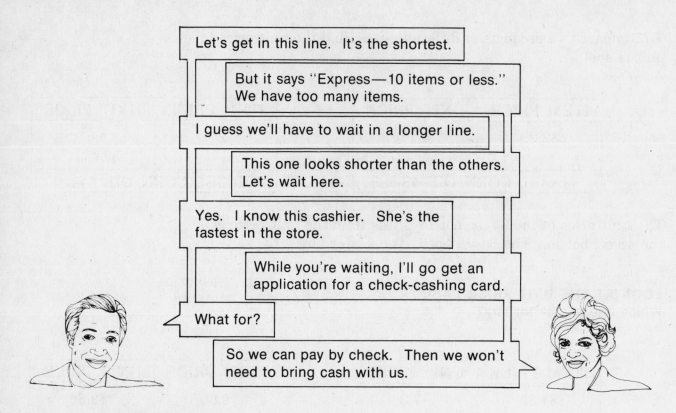

Let's get in this line. It's the shortest.

But it says "Express—10 items or less." We have too many items.

I guess we'll have to wait in a longer line.

This one looks shorter than the others. Let's wait here.

Yes. I know this cashier. She's the fastest in the store.

While you're waiting, I'll go get an application for a check-cashing card.

What for?

So we can pay by check. Then we won't need to bring cash with us.

LISTEN TO THESE PEOPLE.
The customer is using coupons and paying the cashier.

Do you have any coupons?

Yes. Here they are.

Let's see. Sorry, but this one is no good.

How come?

It's expired. It was good only until the end of last month.

Oh. I didn't see the date on it.

And with this one, you have to buy two cans to get the discount.

OK. I'll get another can. Are the others all right?

Yes. Your coupons are worth $1.85. So your total bill comes to $28.36.

LOOK AT THIS APPLICATION.
It is for a check-cashing card.

I.D.# _____

CUSTOMER'S NAME (PRINT)

LAST **Nolan** FIRST **Peter** MIDDLE **J**

ADDRESS   TEL. NO.

15 Park Pl., Houston   **657-1148**

EMPLOYER'S NAME & ADDRESS   TEL. NO.

Walden Products, 25 15ᵗʰ St. **555-1234**

NAME & ADDRESS OF BANK   BANK ACC'T NO.

First State Bank, 102 Main Ave. **1-201-59178**

IDENTIFICATION (LICENSE NO., etc.)

N175482-163-28 (Driver's Lic.)   **Mary**

CUSTOMER'S SIGNATURE   SPOUSE'S NAME

Peter Nolan

APPROVED: GENERAL STORE MANAGER   DATE APPROVED

FILL IN THIS APPLICATION.
Write information about yourself.

I.D.# *290-92-5440*

CUSTOMER'S NAME (PRINT)

LAST *Volovnik* FIRST *Valentina* MIDDLE *S.*

ADDRESS   TEL. NO.

5824 Rhode Island Av. #1, Cinti *631-3489*

EMPLOYER'S NAME & ADDRESS   TEL. NO.

JIIMCO 6418 Vine Street   *242-0087*

NAME & ADDRESS OF BANK   BANK ACC'T NO.

Communicating Arts C.U. P.O.Box 14123 *650449*

IDENTIFICATION (LICENSE NO., etc.)

QE 359944 (State ID)   *Garry*

CUSTOMER'S SIGNATURE   SPOUSE'S NAME

Valentina Volovnik

APPROVED: GENERAL STORE MANAGER   DATE APPROVED

CLOSE-UP ON LANGUAGE

Comparing things

Words that compare only two things are called <u>comparatives</u>:

cheap.............. <u>cheaper</u>   This butter is cheap.

But margarine is <u>cheaper than</u> butter.

pretty.............<u>prettier</u>   Maria is pretty.

But Ann is <u>prettier than</u> Maria.

interesting......<u>more interesting</u>   That book is interesting.

But this book is <u>more interesting than</u> that one.

(Notice the word <u>than</u> in the sentences.)

These words are also <u>comparatives</u>:

good............... <u>better</u>   That orange juice is good.

But this kind of orange juice is <u>better than</u> that kind.

bad.................<u>worse</u>   The traffic is bad.

The traffic on this street is <u>worse than</u> the traffic on the other street.

Words that compare one thing with more than one other thing are called <u>superlatives</u>:

cheap.............. <u>cheapest</u>   This margarine is <u>the cheapest</u> in the store.

pretty.............<u>prettiest</u>   Angela is <u>the prettiest</u> girl I have ever seen.

interesting......<u>most interesting</u>   He is the <u>most interesting</u> teacher in school.

Add <u>est</u> to one-syllable words and words that end with <u>y</u>:

big..................<u>biggest</u>   Tom bought <u>the biggest</u> steak in the store.

small..............<u>smallest</u>   Please buy <u>the smallest</u> jar of mayonnaise.

happy.............<u>happiest</u>   Today is <u>the happiest</u> day of my life.

Use <u>most</u> with words that have more than two syllables:

expensive........<u>most expensive</u>   He bought <u>the most expensive</u> car on the lot.

intelligent...... <u>most intelligent</u> She is <u>the most intelligent</u> person I know.

The superlative forms of good and bad are:

good............... best   This is the best coffee I ever drank.

bad..................worst   This is the worst winter I can remember.

(Notice the word the in the sentences that have superlatives.)

PRACTICE COMPARING THINGS.
Use the examples on the last page to help you decide whether to use the comparative or superlative form.   Use the words than and the where you need to.

A.   Fred is ____the tallest____ person in the class.   (tall)

B.   Wallbrown's has _____ prices in town.   (good)

C.   That brand of coffee is _____ this brand.   (bad)

D.   We waited in _____ _ line in the store.   (short)

E.   The 64-oz. bottle is _____ _____ the 48-oz. bottle.   (expensive)

F.   Orange juice is _____ apple juice.   (good)

G.   I'll carry _____ bag of the two.   (heavy)

H.   Yoko was _____ Carmen in finding a job.   (lucky)

I.   This is the _____ chocolate I ever ate.   (delicious)

J.   Your handwriting is _____ mine.   (bad)

K.   This is the _____ of all the articles in today's paper.   (interesting)

L.   What's _____ sandwich on today's menu?   (tasty)

M.   I am _____ she is.   (old)

N.   She is _____ person I ever met.   (happy)

O.   He is _____ his brother.   (young)

P.   The Millers _____ people we know.   (friendly)

Q.   Please give me a towel that is _____ this one.   (dry)

R.   Miss White's class is _____ one in the school.   (large)

TRY IT ON YOUR OWN.
Write about your family.
Compare the people.
Use words like: old, young, short, tall, fat, thin.

_____

_____

Irregular past tense verbs

Irregular past tense verbs in this unit:

buy.........................bought   eat...........................ate
pay.........................paid   drink.......................drank

Irregular past tense verbs from other units:

say............................ said   make.......................made
have...........................had   take........................ took
do...............................did   get............................got
see.............................saw   meet........................met

PRACTICE USING THESE WORDS.
Use the present or the past tense.
(Use the present when you talk about habits and customs.)

A. We always _____ turkey every Friday. (eat)

B. I _____ more for that last week. (pay)

C. How do you _____ this word? (say)

D. He usually _____ a quart of milk once a week. (buy)

E. I _____ three cups of coffee this morning. (drink)

F. I _____ a check in the mail yesterday. (get)

G. My son _____ his own bed every morning. (make)

H. They _____ an interesting movie last night. (see)

I. He _____ a present for his wife in that store last month. (buy)

J. We _____ a lot of food for breakfast this morning. (eat)

K. Tom says that he _____ enough money to pay the bill. (have)

L. They _____ at school last summer. (meet)

M. He _____ all of that work in just two hours. (do)

N. I called her and she _____ that the job was filled. (say)

O. I _____ a few mistakes on the test. (make)

P. He was late because he _____ the wrong bus. (take)

Q. How much rent do you _____ ? (pay)

R. She _____ her son to school before she goes to work. (take)

S. We _____ the baby a bath after dinner every night. (give)

T. I usually _____ the same bus driver every morning. (see)

58

Making suggestions

Words for making suggestions:

Let's	Let's go shopping this afternoon.
could	We could eat at the Italian restaurant.
How about	How about going to the movies?
Why don't	Why don't you buy a warmer coat?

PRACTICE MAKING SUGGESTIONS.
Use let's, could, how about, or why don't.
Use each one.

A. Suggest having pizza for dinner.

_____

B. Suggest buying a new car.

_____

C. Suggest moving to a bigger apartment.

_____

D. Suggest looking in the newspaper for a job.

_____

E. Suggest going to school to learn English.

_____

F. Suggest visiting a friend.

_____

Imperatives

Use imperatives to tell people what to do.

Write your name.	Ask your teacher.
Close the door.	Listen to the music.
Give me my pen.	Practice your English.
Talk to the teacher.	Look at the picture.
Watch your step.	Keep right.
Pay at the door.	Use handrails.

PRACTICE USING IMPERATIVES.
Tell these people what to do.

A. PERSON: I'm hungry.

YOU: _____ Eat something. _____

B. PERSON: I'm tired.

YOU: _____

C. PERSON: I can't speak English well.

YOU: _____

D. PERSON: I don't know my friend's phone number.

YOU: _____

E. PERSON: I don't have change for the bus.

YOU: _____

F. PERSON: It's dark in this room.

YOU: _____

Position words (prepositions)

Words to tell where something is:

| | above | I live on the second floor. They live <u>above</u> me on the third floor. |
| | below | The floor <u>below</u> me is the first floor. |

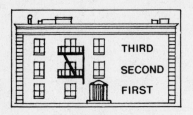

| | under | I found the pen <u>under</u> the table. |
| | on top of | Put the book <u>on top of</u> the table. |

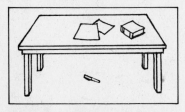

	next to	The seat <u>next to</u> me is empty.
	in front of	I can't see the movie because the person <u>in front of</u> me is very tall.
	in back of	The person <u>in back of</u> me can see because he is taller than <u>I am</u>.

60

to the left of   The muffin mix is <u>to the left of</u> the cookie mix.

to the right of   The cookie mix is <u>to the right of</u> the muffin mix.

PRACTICE USING POSITION WORDS.
Use them in a sentence.

A. _____ (above)

B. _____ (below)

C. _____ (under)

D. _____ (on top of)

E. _____ (next to)

F. _____ (in front of)

G. _____ (in back of)

H. _____ (to the left of)

I. _____ (to the right of)

Write other position words that you know:

_____

PRACTICE ON YOUR OWN

A.   Make a shopping list. Look at the food ads in a newspaper. Find ads for some of the things on your list. Compare the prices from a few of the stores. Which store has the best prices?

B.   Get coupons for some of the things you buy. Look in the newspaper. Look on the containers of the products you use. Redeem your coupons at the store. How much money did you save?

C.   Go to the supermarket. Ask where things are. Find the things you need by following the directions.

D.   Look at the unit pricing information for each product. Which size is the best buy? Do you always buy the product with the lowest unit price?

E.   Apply for a check-cashing card at a store you shop in.

UNIT 3

WOULD YOU LIKE TO TRY IT ON FOR SIZE?

IN THIS UNIT YOU WILL LEARN:

how to ask about and tell about
    intention (going to . . .)
how to ask about and tell about
    needs and wants
how to ask for and give an opinion
how to express approval and disapproval
how to talk about clothing (the
    names of garments)
how to ask for and offer help
how to refuse help
how to fill out an application for
    a charge account

Notice these words and phrases in the unit:

How do you like . . . ?
What do you think of . . . ?
How does this ____ look?   How does it feel?
It feels/looks ____ .   It's very/not becoming.
going to and **will** to talk about
    the future
put in, put on, put down, pick out,
    pick up, look for, look at, try on,
    take off, take out, write down
the verb forms used with singulars
    and plurals (pants fit, skirt fits)
me, you, him, her, us, them
mine, yours, his, hers, ours, theirs

LOOK AT THE PICTURE.
Find these words in the picture.

1. escalator
2. (clothing) rack
3. display case
4. dressing rooms
5. mirror
6. price tag
7. sale table
8. shopping bag
9. sales slip
10. hanger

TALK TOPICS

LOOK AT THE PICTURE.
Talk about what you see.

What is this place?
What can you buy here?
Where do you try things on?
What is a sale table?
How do you get to the other floors?
How can you find out where to find
    things in the store?
How can you find out what size
    you wear?
How do you return something you
    don't want?

What are some differences between
    this picture and the first one?
Talk about what has changed.

ASK ABOUT OTHER THINGS IN THE PICTURE.
Use all of these question words: <u>who</u>, <u>what</u>, <u>where</u>, <u>which</u>, <u>how</u>.
Write your new words.

11. _____   16. _____
12. _____   17. _____
13. _____   18. _____
14. _____   19. _____
15. _____   20. _____

SHOPPING FOR CLOTHES

LISTEN TO THESE PEOPLE.
They are talking about shopping for clothes.

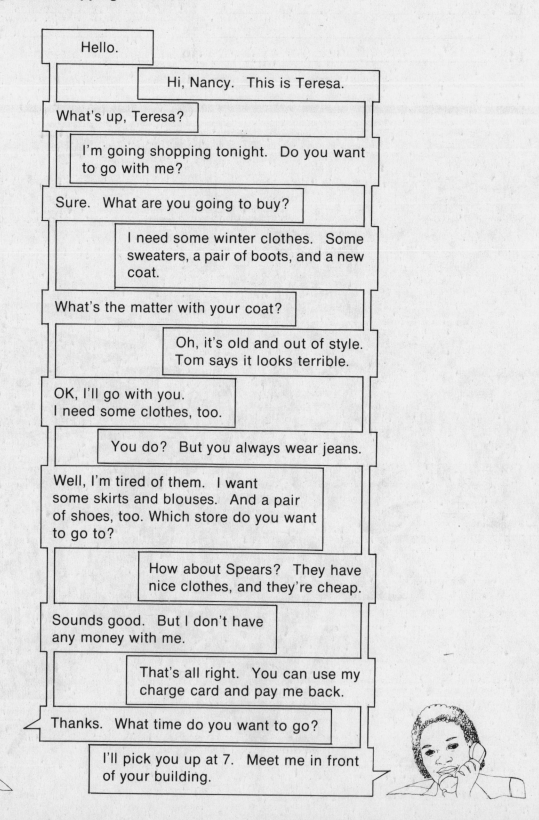

Hello.

Hi, Nancy. This is Teresa.

What's up, Teresa?

I'm going shopping tonight. Do you want to go with me?

Sure. What are you going to buy?

I need some winter clothes. Some sweaters, a pair of boots, and a new coat.

What's the matter with your coat?

Oh, it's old and out of style. Tom says it looks terrible.

OK, I'll go with you.
I need some clothes, too.

You do? But you always wear jeans.

Well, I'm tired of them. I want some skirts and blouses. And a pair of shoes, too. Which store do you want to go to?

How about Spears? They have nice clothes, and they're cheap.

Sounds good. But I don't have any money with me.

That's all right. You can use my charge card and pay me back.

Thanks. What time do you want to go?

I'll pick you up at 7. Meet me in front of your building.

FILL IN THE MISSING WORDS.
Practice talking about shopping for clothes. Use the dialogue on page 66 for help.

LAN: Would you like _____ _____ shopping with _____ ?

LEE: What are you _____ _____ buy?

LAN: I _____ a new suit and _____ shirts.

LEE: I'll _____ with you. I need some _____ , too.

LAN: What _____ of clothes are you _____ to _____ ?

LEE: I need a _____ of shoes, a pair _____ jeans, and

_____ ties.

LAN: Ties? _____ you have so many ties! What's the

_____ with the ones you _____ ?

LEE: They're all _____ _____ style, and I'm _____ of them.

_____ store do you want to _____ to?

LAN: Why don't we go _____ Master's? I have a charge

account there, and _____ have nice _____ .

LEE: _____ good. But I don't have _____ money with me.

LAN: _____ OK. You can _____ my _____ card and pay me

_____ .

LEE: Thanks.

TALK TO THIS PERSON.
Make plans to go shopping together.
Talk about what you want to buy.
Ask about what the other person wants to buy.
What will each of you say?

YOU: _____ (invite)

PERSON: _____ (accept)

YOU: _____ (want/need)

PERSON: _____ (want/need)

YOU: _____ (suggest store)

PERSON: _____ (arrange to meet)

LOOK AT THESE PICTURES.
They show women's clothing.
Write the names of the clothes under the pictures.
Use the clothing list.

_____

_____

_____

_____

_____

_____

_____

_____

_____

_____

_____

_____

_____

_____

_____

_____

CLOTHING LIST (women's clothes)

dress	sweater	boots	nightgown
hat	jacket	pants	bra
coat	skirt	jeans	pantyhose
blouse	gloves	shoes	T-shirt

Write the names of other clothes that women wear:

_____

_____

68

LOOK AT THESE PICTURES.
They show men's clothing.
Write the names of the clothes under the pictures.
Use the clothing list.

_____

_____

_____

_____

_____

_____

_____

_____

_____

_____

_____

_____

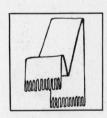

_____

_____

_____

_____

CLOTHING LIST (men's clothes)

belt	undershirt	raincoat	slacks/pants
overcoat	pajamas	undershorts	jacket
robe	shirt	socks	shoes
tie (necktie)	suit	sweater	scarf

Write the names of other clothes that men wear:

_____

_____

LISTEN TO THESE PEOPLE.
They are asking for directions in a department store.

Can I help you?

Yes. Where can I find women's clothing?

What are you looking for?

Well, sweaters . . . blouses . . . skirts . . .

You'll find sweaters, blouses, and skirts in the sportswear department on this floor.

What about coats and shoes?

They're on the second floor. Coats are at the rear, and shoes are next to the elevators.

Thank you. How do we get upstairs?

There's an escalator in the middle of the floor. The elevators are against the far wall, through the men's department.

Thanks.

Excuse me. Where can I find coats?

At the end of this aisle, past the lingerie department, on the right.

Where are the junior coats?

Down this aisle, too. They're on the left.

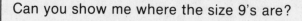

Can you show me where the size 9's are?

They're on the other side of this rack, right across the aisle from the mirror.

And where can I try this on?

The dressing rooms are in the corner behind the cash register.

LOOK AT THIS FLOOR PLAN.
It is the first floor of a department store.

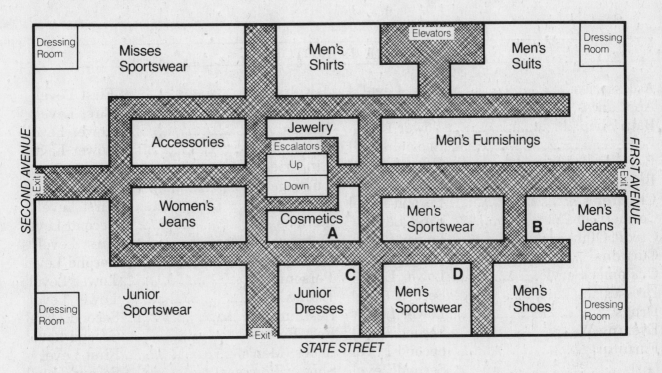

TALK TO THESE PEOPLE.
Tell them how to get to the department
they are looking for.

A. You are a sales clerk in the cosmetics department.

    PERSON: Where can I find the men's shoe department?

        YOU: _____

B. You are a sales clerk in the men's jeans department.

    PERSON: Can you tell me where the women's jeans are?

        YOU: _____

C. You are a sales clerk in the Junior dress department.

    PERSON: How do I get to the men's suit department?

        YOU: _____

D. You are a sales clerk in the men's sportswear department.

    PERSON: Where is the jewelry department?

        YOU: _____

LOOK AT THIS STORE DIRECTORY.
Talk about what you can find in each of the departments.

STORE DIRECTORY

Accessories	First Level	Jewelry	First Level
Appliances	Lower Level	Juniors	First Level
Bath Shop	Lower Level	Lamps	Lower Level
Books	Second Level	Linen	Lower Level
Boys'	Second Level	Lingerie	Second Level
Bridal Shop	Second Level	Luggage	First Level
Children's	Second Level	Men's	First Level
Cosmetics	First Level	Notions	Second Level
Credit Office	Lower Level	Outerwear (Men's)	First Level
Curtains	Lower Level	Outerwear (Women's)	Second Level
Customer Service	Lower Level	Personnel	Lower Level
Dresses	Second Level	Pianos	Lower Level
Drugs	Lower Level	Restaurant	Second Level
Evening Wear	Second Level	Rest Rooms	Second Level
Furniture	Second Level	Shoes (Men's)	First Level
Girls'	Second Level	Shoes (Women's)	Second Level
Handbags	First Level	Sportswear	First Level
Hosiery	Second Level	Stationery	Second Level
Housewares	Lower Level	Swimwear	Second Level
Infants	Second Level	Women's	Second Level

TALK TO THESE PEOPLE.
Tell them where to go in the store.

A. PERSON: I am looking for a shirt for a 10-year-old boy.

YOU: _____

B. PERSON: I want to buy a pair of socks for my mother.

YOU: _____

C. PERSON: I am looking for women's bathing suits.

YOU: _____

D. PERSON: Where do I go to apply for a charge card?

YOU: _____

E. PERSON: Where can I find cookbooks?

YOU: _____

F. PERSON: Where can I apply for a job?

YOU: _____

LOOK AT THE SHOPPING LIST.
Read the list at the bottom of the page.
Write the words under the name of the department in which you will find them.

ACCESSORIES	SPORTSWEAR	COSMETICS
_____	_____	_____
_____	_____	_____
_____	_____	_____
_____	_____	_____

MEN'S FURNISHINGS	LINGERIE	JEWELRY
_____	_____	_____
_____	_____	_____
_____	_____	_____
_____	_____	_____

STATIONERY	SPORTING GOODS	OUTERWEAR
_____	_____	_____
_____	_____	_____
_____	_____	_____

SHOPPING LIST

nightgown	man's raincoat	writing paper	ties
woman's jeans	woman's gloves	woman's scarf	earrings
eye makeup	necklace	pens	woman's golf sweater
man's belt	woman's belt	lipstick	women's underwear
perfume	woman's robe	bowling balls	bracelets
man's gloves	envelopes	man's overcoat	golf clubs
basketball	woman's sweatshirt	handbag	

LISTEN TO THESE PEOPLE.
They are talking about how clothes fit.

What do you think about this coat, Nancy?

It's nice, but it doesn't fit well.

What's the matter with it?

It's too big. Try on a smaller size.

How's this?

It looks too tight. How does it feel?

It feels tight. I guess it's too small.

Take it off and try this one on for size.

OK. How does it look?

It fits well. Do you like it?

Yes, it's perfect. I think I'll get it.

Good. Let's take it over to the cashier.

How do you like this dress, Teresa?

I think it's too long and I don't like that style.

It doesn't feel comfortable, either.

Why don't you try this one on? I think it'll look good on you.

OK.

Well, how does it look?

Oh, great! How does it feel?

It feels very comfortable. Is it too long?

No. It fits just right. It's very becoming.

Really? Then I'll take it.

FILL IN THE MISSING WORDS.
Practice talking about how clothes fit.

A. That dress is too _____ .

   Try on a smaller _____ .

B. Those pants are _____ tight.

   Try on a _____ size.

C. These slacks _____ too long.

   Do you have a pair that is _____ ?

D. The coat _____ just right.

   It's very _____ .

E. This sweater is _____ loose.

   I think I need a _____ size.

FILL IN THE MISSING WORDS.
Practice asking for and giving an opinion.

A. What do you _____ about this hat?

   It _____ good on you.

B. How do you _____ these shoes?

   They look very _____ .

C. How does this dress _____ on me?

   It doesn't _____ you too well.

D. _____ this sweater look _____ on me?

   It looks _____ ! You should _____ it.

E. _____ _____ jeans becoming?

   Yes. _____ look good _____ you.

F. Are these slacks _____ long on me?

   No. They _____ just _____ . They're very

   _____ .

LISTEN TO THESE PEOPLE.
They are talking about men's sizes.

May I help you?

Yes. I'm looking for some shirts and slacks.

What size do you wear?

I'm not sure.

I can measure you if you like.

Thank you.

OK. For shirts we'll need your neck and sleeve measurements. Let's see. Your sleeve length is 31, and your neck measures 14½.

What size is that?

You can take a small, but the sleeves may be too long. Or you can take a 14½–31. The smalls are on the top shelf against the wall, and the 14½–31s are on this table.

Thank you. And can you measure me for slacks?

For slacks, we need your waist size and inseam length. Your waist is 30 inches, and your inseam is also 30.

So what size slacks do I take?

You can buy a 30–30, or a 30 short. Or we will hem them to your length.

Thanks a lot. I'll look at the slacks first. Can I try them on?

Sure. The men's dressing room is right over there.

All measurements are in inches.

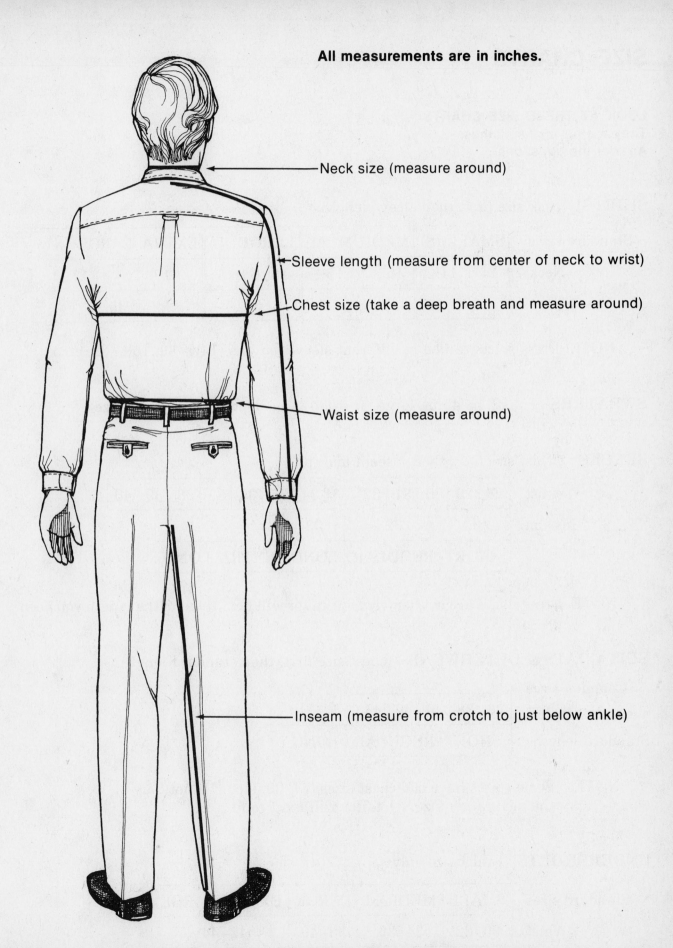

Neck size (measure around)

Sleeve length (measure from center of neck to wrist)

Chest size (take a deep breath and measure around)

Waist size (measure around)

Inseam (measure from crotch to just below ankle)

SIZE CHARTS

LOOK AT THESE SIZE CHARTS.
They are for men's clothes.
Answer the questions.

SHIRTS   (neck size first, then sleeve length):

Standard sizes	SMALL (S)		MEDIUM (M)		LARGE (L)		EXTRA LARGE (XL)	
Neck	14	14½	15	15½	16	16½	17	17½
Sleeve	32		33		34		35	

NOTE: Dress shirts can be in different sleeve lengths (14½–33, 16½–32, etc.)

SWEATERS   (small, medium, large, or extra large depending on shirt size)

SLACKS   (waist size first, then inseam length):

Waist	28	29	30	31	32	33	34	35	36	37	38	39	40
Inseam	30			32			33		36				
	SHORT		REGULAR			LONG		EXTRA LONG				

NOTE: Dress slacks are not hemmed.   A tailor will hem them to the length you need.

SUIT COATS & OUTERWEAR   (chest size first, then standard length):

Common sizes

Chest	36	38	40	42	44
Standard lengths	SHORT		REGULAR		LONG

NOTE: Some stores have odd chest sizes (37, 39, etc.).   If not, buy
the next larger size.   A tailor will fix it to fit.

UNDERSHORTS   (waist size only)

Standard sizes	SMALL	MEDIUM	LARGE	EXTRA LARGE
Waist	30–32	34–36	38–40	42–44

UNDERSHIRTS (chest size only)

Standard sizes	SMALL	MEDIUM	LARGE	EXTRA LARGE
Chest	36	38	40	42

A. You bought a 15½–34 shirt for your father. The neck fits, but the sleeves are a little too long. What size will you try next?

_____

B. Jim tried on a pair of slacks with a 34 waist, but they were just a little too tight. What size should he try on next?

_____

C. A 40 Regular suit fit Mike in the chest and shoulders, but it was too long in the sleeves. What size should he try?

_____

D. A sweater in a size large was a little too loose on you. What size will you try?

_____

TALK TO THIS PERSON.
He is a tailor.
You want him to fix a suit you are buying.
Tell him to make the pants legs narrower and shorter. Tell him to make the waist of the pants tighter, and the sleeves of the jacket longer. What will you say?

TAILOR: Do you like this length for the pants?
YOU: No,_____

TAILOR: The legs seem too wide for you.
YOU: Yes,_____

TAILOR: Is the waist all right?
YOU: No,_____

TAILOR: What about the jacket? Aren't the sleeves too short?
YOU: Yes,_____

TAILOR: OK. I'll take in the legs and shorten them. I'll take in the waist, too. And I'll lengthen the sleeves of the jacket. Your suit will be ready next week.

LOOK AT THESE SIZE CHARTS.
They are for women's clothes.
Answer the questions.

JUNIORS	3	5	7	9	11	13	
MISSES	4	6	8	10	12	14	16
WOMEN (regular) (half size)	18 18½	20 20½	22 22½	24½			
BLOUSES & SWIMSUITS (bust size)	30	32	34	36	38	40	
SWEATERS & SHIRTS	SMALL	MEDIUM	LARGE				
JEANS (waist size)	28	29	30	31	32	33	34
BRAS (chest)	32	34	36	38	40		
(cup)	A	B	C	D			

A. Sue tries on a pair of pants in a Junior size 11, but they are too large. What size will she try next?

_____

B. A Misses size 8 coat is too tight on Carla. What size will she try next?

_____

C. You know that you wear a size 30 blouse. What size will you try on in a sweater?

_____

D. You bought a sweater in a size medium, but it was too small. What size is larger?

_____

E. You try on a pair of jeans in size 32, but they are too loose. What size will you try next?

_____

DESCRIBING CLOTHES

LOOK AT THESE WORDS.
They are used to describe clothing.
Add other words.

MATERIALS	SIZES	COLORS	TEXTURES	PATTERNS
acrylic	small (smaller)	black	soft	striped
cotton	big (bigger)	blue	rough	checked
corduroy	large (larger)	brown	smooth	plaid
denim	short (shorter)	gray	light	polka dots
leather	long (longer)	green	heavy	flowered
nylon	tight (tighter)	orange	_____	
polyester	loose (looser)	purple	_____	
satin	wide (wider)	red	_____	
silk	narrow (narrower)	white		
vinyl		yellow		
wool	_____			
	_____	_____		
_____	_____	_____		
_____	_____	_____		

TALK TO THESE PEOPLE.
Talk to a sales clerk.
Tell the sales clerk what you are looking for. Describe it.
Use words from the lists.

A. I'm looking for a blue cotton shirt with long sleeves.

B. (a jacket) _____

C. (a pair of jeans) _____

D. (a sweater) _____

E. (some gloves) _____

F. (an evening dress) _____

G. (a bathing suit) _____

LISTEN TO THESE PEOPLE.
They are talking about clothing material.

Doesn't this sweater feel soft?

Oh, yes! What's it made of?

The label says it's made of angora and lambswool.

I bet you can't wash it.

You're right. It says, "Dry Clean Only."

Don't buy it. Dry cleaning is too expensive.

This other sweater is washable.

It is? What's it made of?

It's 60% acrylic and 40% wool.
It says, "Machine Wash Cold. Dry Flat."

How does it feel?

It's not as soft as the other one.

Look at this sweater. You can wash it and put it in the dryer.

Really? What's it made of?

100% acrylic. The label says, "Machine Wash Warm. Tumble Dry Low."

I don't like it. It's too stiff and rough.

It'll soften after you wash it.

Do you think so?

Yes. I bought one like that and it was much softer after I washed it.

All right. I think I'll try it on.

LOOK AT THESE CARE LABELS.
They tell you how to care for clothes.
Answer the questions.

A.

100% COTTON
MADE IN HONG KONG
MACHINE WASH COLD
MACHINE DRY COOL
DO NOT BLEACH

1. What is this garment made of?

_____

2. What temperature setting should you use on the washing machine?

_____

B.

MACHINE WASH WARM
TUMBLE DRY LOW
USE COOL IRON
WASH DARK COLORS
SEPARATELY

1. Can you put this garment in the dryer?

_____

2. Why should you "Wash dark colors separately"?

_____

C.

100% SHETLAND WOOL
DRY CLEAN OR
HAND WASH
DRY FLAT

1. Can you put this garment in the washing machine?

_____

2. Can you put this garment in the dryer?

_____

D.

MACHINE WASH WARM
GENTLE CYCLE
DRIP DRY
PRESS WITH COOL
IRON

1. What is the difference between a gentle cycle and a regular cycle?

_____

2. What does "Drip Dry" mean?

_____

E.

80% ARNEL 20% NYLON
MACHINE WASH COLD
NO CHLORINE BLEACH
REMOVE PROMPTLY
LINE DRY

1. What is "Chlorine Bleach?"

_____

2. What does "Remove Promptly" mean?

_____

LISTEN TO THESE PEOPLE.
They are customers and sales clerks.

Can I help you?

No, thank you. I'm just looking.

May I help you?

I'm looking for a present for my husband.

Did you have anything special in mind?

A sweater, maybe.

We have some wool sweaters on sale.

How much are they?

$25 reduced from $38. What color?

How about that bright blue one? Do you have it in a large?

Yes, here it is.

It's very nice. I'll take it.

Will that be cash or charge?

Cash.

Can you help me, please?

Sure. What would you like?

Do you have any cotton T-shirts?

They're on this rack. What color?

I'd like a red one in a medium.

Here you are. Would you like to try it on?

Yes, thanks.

FILL IN THE MISSING WORDS.
Practice talking to a sales clerk.

A. Can I _____ you?

_____ thank you. I'm _____ _____ .

B. May I help _____ ?

Yes. I'm _____ for a present _____ my mother.

Did you _____ something _____ in mind?

I don't know. _____ a silk blouse.

_____ color?

Do _____ have _____ white ones?

Yes, we _____ . What size does your mother _____ ?

I think she _____ a size 40.

Here's a white silk _____ in a _____ 40.

Oh, that's _____ pretty. How _____ is it?

_____ $39.95.

That's pretty expensive, but I'll _____ it anyway.

Fine. Will that be _____ or charge?

TRY IT IN CLASS.
Practice asking a sales clerk for help.
Practice with another student.
One of you is the sales clerk, and the other is
the customer.

A. The customer asks for a garment such as a pair of pants, a shirt, etc.

B. The sales clerk asks about size, color, and material.

C. The customer describes the garment and asks about price.

D. The sales clerk asks if the customer wants to try it on.

E. The customer brings back the garment, says it doesn't fit, and asks for a larger (or smaller) size.

F. After trying it on again, the customer buys (or says he doesn't want) the garment.

LISTEN TO THESE PEOPLE.
They are talking about sales.

Look at these ads. They're having a big sale at Master's.

Really? What's on sale?

Coats, sweaters, wool slacks and skirts; all kinds of winter clothes.

Who wants to buy winter clothes now? It's almost spring.

That's why it's all on sale. They want to get rid of the winter clothes.

But if you buy winter clothes now, you can't wear them until next fall.

That's true, but you can save a lot of money when you buy clothes at the end of the season.

But how do you know what the styles will be next fall?

You don't. But some clothes are always in style. If you buy the right clothes, you can wear them for a few years.

Is that what you do?

Most of the time. Last fall, I bought some clothes for the spring and summer. Do you want to see them?

Sure. And then we can go to Master's and pick out some clothes for next fall and winter.

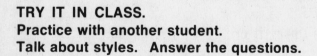

TRY IT IN CLASS.
Practice with another student.
Talk about styles. Answer the questions.

A. What kinds of clothes are in style this year?

B. What clothes were in style last year?

LOOK AT THESE ADS.
They are for sales on clothing.
Answer the questions.

A.

44% to 50% off Men's Dress & Sports Shirts
Orig. 5.99-17.99

Sale **2.99-7.99**

1. What kinds of shirts are on sale?

_____

2. How much can you save on a $17.99 shirt?

_____

B.

37% to 50% off Men's & Young Men's Corduroy Jeans
Orig. 15.99-21.99

Sale **9.99**

1. Can you get denim jeans at the sale price?

_____

2. What was the original price of the jeans?

_____

C.

36% off Women's Large Size Flannel Gowns. Size 42-48.
Orig. 10.99

Sale **6.99**

1. Are all flannel gowns on sale?

_____

2. Can you get a size 14 gown on sale?

_____

D.

Bra irreg., If perf. 4.50-$6

Sale **2/3.99**

1. What kind of bras are on sale?

_____

2. What does "if perf." mean?

_____

3. How much will you pay for 2 bras?

_____

E.

25% to 50% off All Men's Winter Outerwear
Reg. & Orig. 19.99-64.99

Sale **14.99-29.99**

1. What is "outerwear"?

_____

2. What does "Orig. 19.99–64.99" mean?

_____

3. When is winter outerwear on sale?

_____

LOOK AT THIS APPLICATION.
It is for a charge account at a department store.
Fill in information about yourself.

CHARGE ACCOUNT APPLICATION   SPEAR'S

Name _____ Date of Birth _____
     (Last)   (First)   (M.I.)

Address _____
     (Number)   (Street)   (City)   (State)   (Zip)

Phone _____ Rent _____ Own _____

Name of Employer _____

Employer Address _____ Business phone _____

Position _____ Yearly salary _____

Social Security number _____

Name of Bank _____ Account number (checking) _____

Bank Address _____ Account number (savings) _____

Debts: Monthly mortgage payment _____ Rent _____

Outstanding Loans: Original balance _____ Remaining balance _____

     Monthly payments _____

Other charge accounts (include account number):

1. _____ 3. _____

2. _____ 4. _____

I authorize the firm to which this application is made or any
investigative agency to investigate the information provided about my
credit and financial responsibility.

Date _____ _____
                                              Signature of Applicant

CLOSE-UP ON LANGUAGE

Talking about the future

Notice the ways you can talk about the future in English.

A. With <u>going to</u>:

    I'm <u>going to buy</u> a new coat next week.
    We're <u>going to eat</u> at Mario's tonight.

B. With <u>will</u>:

    <u>I will</u> (I'll) <u>buy</u> the coat next week.
    <u>They will</u> (they'll) <u>bring</u> their books tomorrow.

C. With BE + <u>ing</u>:

    <u>She's taking</u> the test this afternoon.
    <u>You're meeting</u> my family next month.

D. With <u>will</u> + BE + <u>ing</u>:

    <u>I'll be talking</u> to you in a few days.
    <u>He'll be calling</u> you later this evening.

PRACTICE TALKING ABOUT THE FUTURE.
Look at the first sentence.
Write three other sentences to express the future.

A. We're having a test tomorrow.

                We're going to have a test tomorrow.
               We'll be having a test tomorrow.
                We'll have a test tomorow.

B. I'm leaving at 5:00.

    _____

    _____

    _____

C. He'll bring you a present when he returns.

_____

_____

_____

D. They'll eat dinner at the Italian restaurant tonight.

_____

_____

_____

E. She's going to talk to Mr. Johnson in the morning.

_____

_____

_____

F. Are you driving home later?

_____

_____

_____

G. I'm working late this evening.

_____

_____

_____

H. Will you be paying by check?

_____

_____

_____

I. I'm going to look for a new job next month.

_____

_____

_____

Prepositions with verbs

Notice how these prepositions and verbs go together:

put in	How many dimes did you <u>put in</u>?
put on	<u>Put on</u> your coat.
put down	<u>Put down</u> what you need on this shopping list.
pick out	I want to <u>pick out</u> a nice present.
pick up	Can you <u>pick up</u> a quart of milk on your way home?
look for	I'm <u>looking for</u> a red sweater.
look at	Would you like to <u>look at</u> some shirts?
try on	You can <u>try on</u> the skirt in the fitting room.
try out	Can I <u>try out</u> your new typewriter?
take off	Can I help you <u>take off</u> your coat?
take out	He is <u>taking out</u> his wallet to pay the bill.

Words may come between the verb and the preposition:

<u>Put</u> your coat <u>on</u> before you go out.
<u>Put</u> your number <u>down</u> on this paper.
<u>Try</u> the shoes <u>on</u> before you buy them.
<u>Did</u> you <u>take</u> this book <u>out</u> of the library?

PRACTICE USING VERBS WITH PREPOSITIONS.
Write the verb and the preposition that goes with it.

A. Please _____ your boots _____ in the hall. (take)

B. I _____ this blouse _____ for my mother. (pick)

C. She _____ _____ all of the hats in the store. (look)

D. I want to _____ your address _____ in my notebook. (put)

E. He _____ a dime _____ of his pocket and gave it to her. (take)

F. Would you _____ _____ my dress from the cleaners for me? (pick)

G. We _____ _____ you at school yesterday. (look)

H. Do you want to _____ the sweater _____ for size? (try)

I. Please _____ your money _____ your pocket. (put)

J. Did you _____ _____ the new coffeemaker yet? (try)

K. I want you to _____ another record _____ the record player. (put)

L. Will you help me _____ _____ my glasses? (look)

SUBJECT-VERB AGREEMENT

With a singular noun
use a singular verb:

With a plural noun
use a plural verb:

The <u>book is</u> good.

The <u>books are</u> good.

SINGULAR

PLURAL

The <u>skirt fits</u> well.
The <u>coat looks</u> good on you.
My <u>hat is</u> very warm.

The <u>sleeves fit</u> well.
These <u>shoes look</u> beautiful.
My <u>gloves are</u> very comfortable.

Pants, slacks, shorts, and glasses take a plural verb
except when they are used with the word <u>pair</u>:

This <u>pair</u> of pants <u>is</u> too short.

These <u>pants are</u> too long.

PRACTICE USING THE SINGULAR AND PLURAL FORMS OF VERBS.
Write the form of the verb that agrees with the subject.

A. Those <u>jeans</u> _____ too tight on you.   (be)

B. This <u>sweater</u> _____ very soft.   (feel)

C. My old <u>coat</u> _____ me better than my new one.   (fit)

D. These <u>boots</u> _____ me well.   (fit)

E. That <u>pair</u> of glasses _____ $100.00.   (cost)

F. My <u>glasses</u> only _____ $60.00.   (cost)

G. This <u>shirt</u> _____ your slacks very well.   (match)

H. This <u>belt</u> _____ well with that skirt.   (go)

I. These <u>shoes</u> _____ perfectly with my gray suit.   (go)

J. My <u>sneakers</u> _____ very comfortable.   (feel)

K. Dark <u>colors</u> _____ you look older.   (make)

L. That <u>dress</u> _____ great on you.   (look)

M. The <u>waist</u> of these slacks _____ too loose.   (be)

N. That <u>style</u> _____ you look too fat.   (make)

O. The <u>sleeves</u> on that shirt _____ too long.   (look)

P. This <u>pair</u> of gloves _____ my new coat.   (match)

Q. Wool <u>gloves</u> _____ your hands warm.   (keep)

R. My <u>raincoat</u> _____ me nice and dry.   (keep)

PRONOUNS

Subject pronouns: <u>I</u>, <u>you</u>, <u>he</u>, <u>she</u>, <u>we</u>, <u>they</u>, it
Subject pronouns tell who or what the sentence is about:

Henry writes to Anna once a week.   <u>He</u> writes to Anna once a week.
The women meet outside after work.   <u>They</u> meet outside after work.
The train leaves at 10.   <u>It</u> leaves at 10.

Object pronouns: <u>me</u>, <u>you</u>, <u>him</u>, <u>her</u>, <u>us</u>, <u>them</u>
Notice how object pronouns are used in these sentences:

Henry writes to <u>her</u> once a week.
The girls saw <u>them</u> yesterday.
Yoko told <u>me</u> about it.

PRACTICE USING PRONOUNS.
Choose the pronoun that fits into the sentences.

A. My parents and _____ came to the United States together. (I, me)

B. _____ wants to come over tonight after dinner. (He, Him)

C. You and _____ can meet for lunch tomorrow. (I, me)

D. I want to invite _____ for dinner. (he, him)

E. My parents brought _____ with them. (I, me)

F. Do you want to take a picture of _____ ? (she, her)

G. Could you show _____ some wool sweaters? (we, us)

H. You and _____ look good in this picture. (she, her)

I. The sales clerk asked if _____ wanted to see some sweaters. (we, us)

J. Alan said that he wants to talk to you and _____ . (I, me)

K. Did _____ see you at the party? (they, them)

L. Is _____ the teacher? (he, him)

M. I didn't notice _____ in the dark. (they, them)

N. I never met _____ before. (he, him)

O. The taxi almost ran _____ down on the street. (we, us)

P. Will you write _____ tomorrow? (she, her)

Q. I don't think _____ know each other. (we, us)

R. Please tell me when _____ gets here. (she, her)

S. We gave _____ Tony's phone number. (they, them)

Possessive pronouns: <u>mine</u>, <u>yours</u>, <u>his</u>, <u>hers</u>, <u>ours</u>, <u>theirs</u>

<u>My</u> coat is blue.   The blue coat is <u>mine</u>.
Isn't <u>your</u> jacket red?   Isn't the red jacket <u>yours</u>?
Are these <u>our</u> packages?   Are these packages <u>ours</u>?

REWRITE THESE SENTENCES.
Use these words: <u>mine</u>, <u>yours</u>, <u>his</u>, <u>hers</u>, <u>ours</u>, <u>theirs</u>

A. <u>Her</u> skirt is yellow.

                              The yellow one is hers.
_____

B. <u>Their</u> apartment is at the end of the hall.

_____

C. Isn't <u>your</u> coat green?

_____

D. <u>Their</u> car is black.

_____

E. I think those are <u>our</u> seats.

_____

F. <u>My</u> hat is on the top shelf.

_____

PRACTICE ON YOUR OWN

A. Fill in your sizes if you are a man, or fill in the sizes of a man you know.

Shirt size _____   Sweater size _____
Slacks size _____   Suit size _____
Coat size _____   Undershorts size _____

B. Fill in your sizes if you are a woman, or fill in the sizes of a woman you know.

Dress size _____   Jeans size _____
Blouse size _____   Skirt size _____
Sweater size _____   Coat size _____

C. Practice with a friend. Play a guessing game. One person describes what someone in the room is wearing. The other person tries to guess who it is. For example: "Who is wearing an orange shirt and striped pants?"

D. Visit a department store. Look at the directory.
Find these departments in the store:

> Accessories
> Lingerie
> Children's clothing
> Men's suits
> Juniors
> Women's dresses

E. Ask a clerk to help you find clothes in your size.
If the clothes don't fit, tell the clerk what you need. (Use words like: shorter, longer, smaller, larger, looser, narrower, wider.)

F. Look at your clothes at home.
Use the words on page 81 to describe them.

Sweaters: _____

Shirts or blouses: _____

Slacks: _____

Shoes: _____

Coats and jackets: _____

G. How do you return purchases to a department store?
What papers must you keep?
When can you return what you bought?

H. Look at care labels in your clothes.
Talk about what the directions mean.

UNIT 4

HAVE YOU RENTED THE APARTMENT?

IN THIS UNIT YOU WILL LEARN:

how to ask for a reason (why)
how to give a reason (because)
how to use must, need and have to
how to ask if something is available
    (is there, are there)
how to say that something is available
    (there is, there are)
how to ask for an explanation
    (what does it mean?, what is it about?)
how to talk about a problem (complain)
how to read and understand apartment ads
how to read an apartment floor plan
how to understand a lease

Notice these words and phrases in the unit:

questions with **why**
answers with **because**
there is, there are, is there, are there,
    there isn't, there aren't
turn on, try out, ask about, look for,
    look at, listen for
present perfect tense (**has** or **have** + verb)
if in sentences

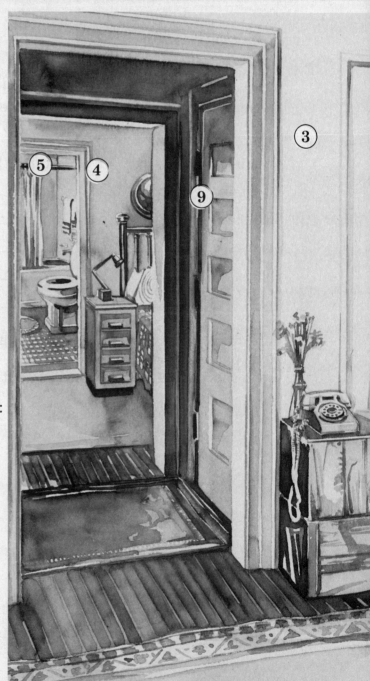

LOOK AT THE PICTURE.
Find these things in the picture.

1. landlord
2. tenant
3. living room
4. bedroom
5. bathroom

6. kitchen
7. refrigerator
8. stove
9. closet
10. cabinets

TALK TOPICS

LOOK AT THE PICTURES.
Talk about what you see.

What is this place?
What are the names of the different
    rooms?
Which person do you think is the landlord?
What do you think the landlord and the
    people are talking about?

What do you think happened to the
    people who lived here?
What is the man on the ladder doing?
    Why?
Why do you think these other people are
    here?
What should be fixed in the apartment?
Who should pay for the repairs?

ASK ABOUT OTHER THINGS IN THE PICTURE.
Use what, where, who, how, which, and why.
Write your new words.

11. _____   16. _____
12. _____   17. _____
13. _____   18. _____
14. _____   19. _____
15. _____   20. _____

LISTEN TO THESE PEOPLE.
They are talking about renting an apartment.

You know, Mike, I have to find an apartment.

Why?

I'm living with my mother in a one-bedroom apartment. I have to sleep in the living room. I need a place of my own.

Can you afford it?

I think so. I bring home $680 a month.

They say you should spend about 40% of that on housing. That's about $272. But you'll need some of that for utilities.

Utilities?

Electricity, gas, and telephone. You'll need about $30 or $40 a month.

So that leaves $232 to $242 for rent. That's not much.

No, but you may be able to find a one-room apartment for that.

That's big enough for me. Then I won't need too much furniture.

Have you saved any money for the security and the first month's rent?

Why do I need money for security?

Because the landlord wants to hold a deposit to pay for damages. It's usually a month's rent.

Well, I've saved about $600. I'll have just enough. Will I get the security back?

If there are no damages when you move out.

FILL IN THE MISSING WORDS.
Practice using have to, must, and need.

A. You may _____ give a month's rent as a security deposit.

B. You _____ furniture for an apartment.

C. You _____ have enough money to pay for the utilities.

D. You _____ pay the rent at the beginning of the month.

E. You'll _____ to save up before you can get an apartment.

F. You'll _____ pay for damages.

TALK TO THESE PEOPLE.
Practice answering questions with because.

A. PERSON: Why do you need a new apartment?

    YOU: _____

B. PERSON: Why do you have to pay a security deposit?

    YOU: _____

C. PERSON: Why did you get such a small apartment?

    YOU: _____

D. PERSON: Why are you still living with your parents?

    YOU: _____

E. PERSON: Why are you saving your money?

    YOU: _____

TRY IT IN CLASS.
Practice with another student.
One student asks a question with why. The other
student answers with a sentence beginning with because.

A.   YOU: _____ (save money)

    PERSON: _____

B.   YOU: _____ (go to school)

    PERSON: _____

LOOK AT THESE ADS.
They are newspaper ads for apartments.
Answer the questions.

A.

ALLENVILLE—3 rms.
E. 18 St. Lux bldg.
Working cpl. pref.
$405 gas incl.
near transp.
Broker   455-3322

1. How many rooms are there in this apartment?

_____

2. What utility is included in the rent?

_____

B.

HIGH HILLS—5½ rms.
2 fam hse. nr. shop.
½ blk. to subway.
$375 utilities incl.
Call owner   277-7575

1. What kind of building is this apartment in?

_____

2. How far away is transportation?

_____

C.

KING HTS.—4 rms.
elev. bldg. 4th fl.
$300/mo. 2 mos. sec.
1 mo. rent. 1 yr. lease.
Wrkng. adults pref.
Owner.   773-3271   9am–5pm

1. How much security deposit must you pay?

_____

2. How many years is the lease?

_____

D.

RIVER PK.—5 rms.
3 lg. bdrms.
child ok. new kit.,
mod. bath, wash. mach.
nr. shopping, schools,
& transit. $450/mo.
gd. area   595-3445 eves.

1. Can children live in this apartment?

_____

2. Does the apartment have a new bathroom?

_____

E.

GRAND ST. 250 betw 18&19.
5 lg. rms. excel. loc.
intercom security system.
A/C. Elev. bldg. clean,
quiet. See supt. on prem.
or call 899-9175 days

1. What kind of building is this apartment in?

_____

2. What is the address of the building?

_____

LOOK AT THESE ABBREVIATIONS.
Match the abbreviations with the words.

apt.	bathroom
bldg.	block
util.	house
kit.	apartment
bath.	large
rms.	rooms
lg.	building
hse.	modern
bdrm.	utilities
mod.	near
incl.	kitchen
nr.	included
blk.	bedroom

FILL IN THE MISSING WORDS.
Practice using the words: rent, utilities, security, landlord, tenants, lease.

A. A _____ is the owner of a rental building or house.

B. People pay _____ each month to the owner.

C. Gas and electricity are _____ .

D. An owner usually asks for _____ to pay for damages.

E. A _____ is an agreement between the owner and people who

are renting the apartment.

F. _____ are people living in a rented apartment.

G. Sometimes the rent includes _____ .

H. If there are no damages, you'll get the _____

back when you move out.

I. Most landlords ask _____ to sign a _____ before

moving in.

J. The _____ must paint the apartment for a new tenant.

LISTEN TO THESE PEOPLE.
They are asking and answering questions about an apartment.

I'm calling about the apartment for rent.

I'm sorry. It's already rented.

I'm calling about the apartment for rent.

Yes. Do you have any questions?

Does the rent include utilities?

It includes gas. You must pay for electricity.

Is there an elevator in the building?

No, there isn't.

Are there laundry facilities?

Yes. There's a washer and dryer in the basement.

Is there transportation nearby?

There's a bus on the corner.

Is there a lease?

Yes, a two-year lease.

When is the apartment available?

June 1st.

When can I see it?

Anytime.

How about tomorrow evening at six?

OK. The address is 609 Holly Lane. My name's Oscar Lopez.

Thank you, Mr. Lopez.

FILL IN THE MISSING WORDS.
Practice asking and answering questions about apartments.

ANGELA: I'm _____ about the apartment _____

OSCAR: Yes. Do you have _____ questions?

ANGELA: How _____ is the rent?

OSCAR: $450 a month.

ANGELA: Does it _____ utilities?

OSCAR: Yes, it _____ gas and electricity.

ANGELA: _____ _____ any air conditioners?

OSCAR: Yes, _____ one in the living room.

ANGELA: _____ _____ washers and dryers?

OSCAR: There's a _____ room on each floor.

ANGELA: _____ _____ a lease?

OSCAR: Yes, a three- _____ lease.

ANGELA: Are there schools _____ ?

OSCAR: The nearest _____ is about a mile away. But

the _____ bus stops _____ the corner.

ANGELA: _____ is the apartment _____ ?

OSCAR: It's _____ right away.

ANGELA: When _____ I see _____ ?

OSCAR: How _____ this evening after six?

ANGELA: Fine. What's the _____ ?

OSCAR: 400 Central Street. I'm in _____ 102.

ANGELA: My name is Angela Martinez.

OSCAR: Thank you, _____ .

TRY IT IN CLASS.
Practice with another student.
Ask about the other person's apartment or house.
Ask about schools, shopping, and transportation.

YOU: _____

PERSON: _____

LISTEN TO THESE PEOPLE.
The landlord is showing the apartment to Rick.

Have you just painted? I smell fresh paint.

Yes, my wife and I cleaned and painted last weekend.

Are there any bugs?

We haven't seen any. It's very clean.

Good. How many closets are there?

Three. One in the hall and two in the bedroom.

Are there screens for the windows?

Yes. They're in the closet.

May I see the kitchen?

Sure. This way, please.

Are the appliances in good condition?

Yes. Would you like to try them?

How do you turn on the oven?

This way. Push in the knob and turn.

Is the refrigerator new?

Yes. We bought it just last year.

Where's the bathroom?

In the hall next to the closet.

Oh. There's no bathtub.

No, only a shower.

Well, thank you for your time. I'll think it over and call you tomorrow evening.

All right. Thanks for coming.

TALK TO THESE PEOPLE.
Practice asking questions about an apartment.
Use the clues at the ends of the blanks.

A.   YOU: _____ (just painted?)

     LANDLORD: Yes.   The apartment is freshly painted.

B.   YOU: _____ (bugs?)

     LANDLORD: No.   We haven't had any bugs.

C.   YOU: _____ (closets?)

     LANDLORD: There's a walk-in closet in the hall, and a linen closet
next to the bathroom.   There are two closets
in the bedroom.

D.   YOU: _____ (appliances?)

     LANDLORD: They're almost new.   Would you like to try them?

E.   YOU: _____ (laundry room?)

     LANDLORD: No, but there is a laundromat a few blocks from here.

F.   YOU: _____ (you pay utilities?)

     LANDLORD: Yes.   Utilities are included.

TRY IT IN CLASS.
Practice with another student.
Read this ad. One person asks the questions
and the other answers them.

**HILLDALE 6rms.
3 bdrms. mod kit.
w/dwshr. sep. entr.
Child OK. no pets.
a/c elev. bldg.
nr. shop. schools &
transp. Ownr. 324-6234**

YOU: _____

PERSON: _____

YOU: _____

PERSON: _____

LOOK AT THIS FLOOR PLAN.
It is for an apartment.

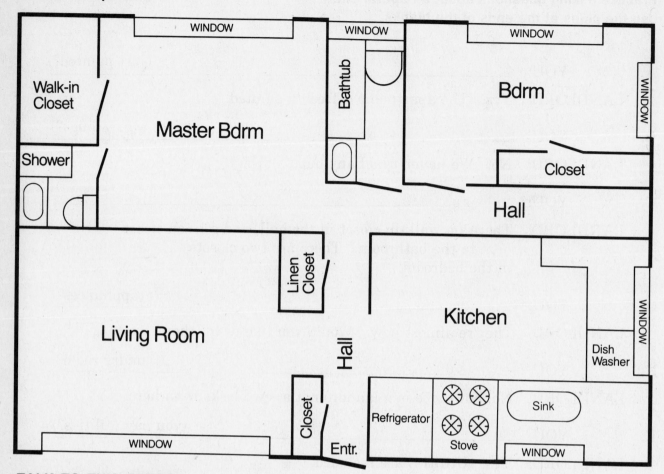

TALK TO THIS PERSON.
Tell about the apartment in the floor plan.
(The kitchen is counted as a room.)

A. PERSON: How many rooms are there?

  YOU: _____ (name the rooms)

B. PERSON: How many bathrooms are there?

  YOU: _____ (tell about them)

C. PERSON: Are there many closets?

  YOU: _____ (tell where they are)

D. PERSON: How's the kitchen?

  YOU: _____ (describe the appliances)

E. PERSON: Are there many windows?

  YOU: _____ (tell where they are)

LOOK AT THE FLOOR PLAN AGAIN.
Answer these questions.   Use these directions:
on the right, on the left, straight ahead, down the hall.
(You may use more than one.)

A.   You are walking through the entrance to the apartment.
Where is the kitchen?

_____Down the hall and on the right._____

B.   You are walking out of the kitchen.   Where is the living room?

_____

C.   You are walking out of the living room.   Where is the linen
closet?

_____

D.   You are standing in front of the linen closet.   Where is
the bathroom?

_____

E.   You are walking out of the larger bathroom.   Where is the
master bedroom?

_____

F.   You are walking out of the master bedroom.   Where is the
smaller bedroom?

_____

G.   You are walking out of the smaller bedroom.   Where is the
entrance to the apartment?

_____

TRY IT IN CLASS.
Practice with another student.
Describe your home or the home of a friend.

_____ (the bedrooms)

_____ (the closets)

_____ (the appliances)

_____ (the bathroom)

LISTEN TO THESE PEOPLE.
They are talking about the neighborhood.

How's the neighborhood?

Nice. It's very safe and quiet.

Is there parking?

You have to park on the street. But it's not too hard to find a space.

What about shopping?

There are a lot of stores about four blocks away.

Is there a supermarket in the area?

Yes, there are two. One is four blocks away and the other is about ten blocks.

Is there transportation nearby?

There are several buses within walking distance.

Are there any schools in the neighborhood?

There's an elementary school just across the street. The junior high and high schools are about a mile away.

Any parks?

There's a small playground next to the elementary school The larger parks are not very near. You'd have to drive.

Are there any recreational facilities?

There's a movie theater in the shopping center and a bowling alley. There's an ice skating rink about a mile away and a swimming pool there, too.

Sounds like a nice neighborhood.

I think so. That's why I moved here.

110

TALK TO THIS PERSON.
Practice asking questions about the neighborhood.
Talk about why you might ask these questions.

A. YOU: _____ (safe?)

    PERSON: It's very safe.   We have a very low crime rate.

B. YOU: _____ (parking?)

    PERSON: You can rent the garage for $35 a month or you can
    park on the street.

C. YOU: _____ (shopping?)

    PERSON: There's a big shopping center within walking distance.

D. YOU: _____ (schools?)

    PERSON: There are no schools nearby.   But the school bus stops
    down the block.

E. YOU: _____ (children?)

    PERSON: There are not too many little kids in the neighborhood.
    There are mostly older adults and families with teenagers.

F. YOU: _____ (parks?)

    PERSON: There's a beautiful large park about a mile from here.

G. YOU: _____ (recreation facilities?)

    PERSON: There's a bowling alley and a movie
    theater in the shopping center.

TRY IT IN CLASS.
Practice with another student.
Tell about your neighborhood.
One person asks the questions and the other answers them.

YOU: _____ (safe?)

PERSON: _____

YOU: _____ (stores?)

PERSON: _____

YOU: _____ (schools?)

PERSON: _____

LOOK AT THIS APARTMENT CHECKLIST.
It tells you what to look for when you shop for a
new apartment.
Fill in the missing words on the checklist.
Some words you can use are: turn on, open and close,
try, ask, look for, look at, listen for, talk to.

APARTMENT CHECKLIST

KITCHEN
_____ all of the appliances.

_____ the oven.

_____ the refrigerator.

_____ the hot and cold water faucets.

_____ the cabinet doors and drawers.

BATHROOM
_____ the faucets in the sink and bathtub (or shower).

_____ the toilet.

HEATING
_____ the heaters or radiators (even in summer).

WINDOWS
_____ all of the windows. Do they work well?

_____ about screens and storm windows.

_____ broken windows and windows that don't open
or close.

WALLS
_____ the paint. (Is it clean and fresh-looking?)

_____ peeling paint, water marks, large cracks.

DOORS
_____ all of the doors. Do they work well?

_____ the locks to make sure they work.

THE BUILDING
_____ dirt and signs of rats and roaches.

_____ noises and be aware of bad smells.

_____ other people who live in the building.

NEIGHBORHOOD
_____ some people who live there.

TALK TO THIS PERSON.
He is a tenant in the building you want to move into.
Practice asking questions about the building and the neighborhood.

A.   YOU: I hope I'm not bothering you. Could I ask you a few questions?
   PERSON: What about?

B.   YOU: Well, I'm thinking about moving into this building. Could
          you tell me about it?
   PERSON: What would you like to know?

C.   YOU: _____ (noise?)

   PERSON: It's a little noisy during the day. But at night it's
          usually quiet.

D.   YOU: _____ (bugs?)

   PERSON: They spray once a month. We haven't had a problem with bugs.

E.   YOU: _____ (clean?)

   PERSON: Yes. The building is kept very clean.

F.   YOU: _____ (repairs?)

   PERSON: They're pretty good about repairs. But sometimes
          you have to wait a couple of days before they fix
          something.

G.   YOU: _____ (security?)

   PERSON: There's a lock on the door to the building.
          You need a key to get in.

H.   YOU: _____ (safe streets?)

   PERSON: The neighborhood's pretty safe. I don't go out much
          at night, though. But I haven't heard about any
          crimes around here.

I.   YOU: _____ (shopping expensive?)

   PERSON: The stores in the neighborhood are pretty expensive.
          I usually drive to the shopping center
          to do my shopping.

J.   YOU: _____

   PERSON: You're welcome.

LISTEN TO THESE PEOPLE.
They are talking about signing a lease and paying the security.

Hello, Mr. Lopez? This is Rick Silver. I've decided to rent your apartment.

OK. Why don't you come over tomorrow evening to sign the lease?

What does the lease say?

Basically, it says that you agree to live in the apartment for a year, to take care of it, to pay for damage, and not to keep any pets.

Is it all right if I bring a friend along to help me read the lease?

It's all right with me. What time will you come?

How about 7?

Fine. Don't forget to bring $450 with you. $225 for the first month's rent and $225 for the security deposit.

Will you return the security deposit?

I'll keep it until you move out. You'll get it back if there are no damages.

Do I have to pay for everything that goes wrong?

Not for normal wear and tear like a leaking faucet. Only if you cause the damage.

I see. And will I be able to go through the apartment tomorrow to make sure everything's all right?

Sure. We can do that tomorrow.

See you tomorrow at 7, Mr. Lopez.

So long, Mr. Silver.

114

LOOK AT THIS LEASE.
Read it with your teacher.
Answer the questions.

The **Tenant** agrees to:

1. Pay rent in the amount of $225.00 on the first day of each month for a period of 12 months.
2. Keep the premises quiet and orderly, not playing televisions, radios, phonographs, or other musical instruments in such a way that it disturbs other tenants.
3. Take good care of the premises and to pay for damages resulting from the tenant's misuse or neglect—except for repairs due to normal wear and tear.
4. Make no alterations, decorations, additions, or improvements in or to the premises without the written consent of the Landlord.
5. Keep no dogs or other animals on the premises without the written permission of the Landlord.

The **Landlord** agrees to:

1. Provide adequate hot and cold water at all times.
2. Provide heat as the law requires.
3. Make all repairs due to normal wear and tear on the premises within a reasonable amount of time.

A. When must the rent be paid?

_____

B. Who must pay for repairs due to normal wear and tear?

_____

C. What must the landlord provide?

_____

D. What must the tenant do before making alterations (changes) in the apartment?

_____

E. Who must pay for repairs needed because of the tenant's neglect or misuse?

_____

LISTEN TO THESE PEOPLE.
They are talking about moving in.

Now that you've signed the lease, Mr. Silver, you can move in any time.

I'll probably move in on the weekend.

Don't forget to have the electricity changed to your name.

How do I do that?

Just call the Electric Company and they'll set up an account in your name. I've already called them to read the meter. If you call right away they won't turn it off.

Who's paying for the electricity now?

I am. I needed the light for painting and for showing the apartment to people.

I'll need to call the Telephone Company, too.

Do you have a lot of furniture?

No. I only have a TV, a small table, two chairs, a dresser, and a bed.

All right, Rick. I'll see you on Saturday.

I'm looking forward to it.

LOOK AT THESE SENTENCES.
They tell what Rick did before moving into a new apartment.
They are in the wrong order.
Number them from 1 to 6 in the order they happened.

_____ He signed a lease and paid a security deposit.

_____ He called about the apartment.

_____ He called the Electric and Telephone Companies.

_____ He found an ad in the newspaper for an apartment for rent.

__1__ Rick figured out how much he could afford to spend on rent.

_____ He looked at the apartment and asked questions about it.

116

FILL OUT THIS QUESTIONNAIRE.
Write in information about your apartment or the apartment of a friend.

1. What floor is the apartment on? _____

2. Is there an elevator in the building? _____

3. How many rooms are there in the apartment? _____

4. How many bathrooms are there? _____

5. How many bedrooms? _____

6. How many closets? _____

7. Is there a dishwasher? _____

8. Is heat included in the rent? _____

9. Are any other utilities included in the rent? _____

   If yes, which ones? _____

   If not, which ones do you pay for? _____

10. Is the building clean? _____

11. Are there any bugs? _____

12. Are the repairs done quickly and well? _____

13. Is there a lot of noise in the building? _____

14. Are there laundry facilities in the building? _____

15. Is the apartment near shopping and transportation? _____

16. What is good about the neighborhood? _____

    _____

17. What is not good about the neighborhood?

    _____

18. What would you like to change in the apartment or in the

    building?

    _____

    _____

19. If you were looking for a new apartment, what would you

    want?

    _____

    _____

LISTEN TO THESE PEOPLE.
They are calling the landlord to complain.

Hello, this is Kim Luck calling. I'm one of your tenants. I have a problem.

Yes. What is it?

There's no heat or hot water in my apartment.

I know. The furnace isn't working. It'll be fixed by tomorrow.

Mr. Lopez? This is Teresa Brown. The toilet is overflowing. My bathroom is flooded.

How did it happen?

My son threw some toys into it.

I'm sorry, but that's not my responsibility.

How come?

Because your son caused the damage, so you must call the plumber. It says so in your lease.

Can you give me the name of a plumber?

Sure. Hold on a minute.

Mr. Lopez? This is Tran Hong. The refrigerator isn't working.

What did you do to it?

Mr. Lopez, you know that it's very old!

I'll send someone to look at it tomorrow.

Tomorrow! But all my food will spoil!

I'm sorry. It's late. There's nothing I can do now.

FILL IN THE MISSING WORDS.
Practice complaining to the landlord.

A. Hello. _____ is Yoko Akiyama. I'm one of your _____ .

Yes. What's the _____ ?

There's no _____ in my apartment. I'm freezing.

OK. I'll _____ someone to look _____ it.

B. Hello. This _____ Kwang Koo. I _____ a problem.

_____ is it?

The lights are not _____ . I have _____ electricity.

All right. I'll _____ someone to look into it.

C. Mrs. Kay? The roof _____ leaking. My kitchen is getting _____ .

How did it _____ ?

I _____ know. Please send _____ to fix it.

You'll have to wait until tomorrow.

_____ ! But my furniture _____ be ruined!

I'm _____ I can't do anything _____ . It's _____ .

TALK TO THIS PERSON.
Practice with another student.
One student is the tenant.
The other person is the landlord.

A. The tenant calls up to complain that the oven
is not working. What will the tenant say? What will
the landlord say?

TENANT: My oven isn't working.

LANDLORD: _____

TENANT: No, I didn't do anything to damage it.

LANDLORD: _____

B. The tenant calls to complain about a closet door that
fell off. What will the tenant say? What will the landlord say?

TENANT: _____

LANDLORD: _____

CLOSE-UP ON LANGUAGE

The present perfect tense

I have lived (I've lived)
You have lived (you've lived)
He has lived (he's lived)
She has lived (she's lived)
We have lived (we've lived)
They have lived (they've lived)

I've lived here for two years.
You've lived there for a long time.
He's lived here a year.
She's lived in many places.
We've always lived here.
They've lived here before.

PRACTICE USING THE PRESENT PERFECT TENSE.
Use have or has and the correct form of the verb.

A. I _____ a lot of money. (save)

B. We _____ the living room. (paint)

C. He _____ the lease. (sign)

D. She _____ the apartment already. (see)

E. They _____ in a few buildings. (look)

F. You _____ to her a few times. (talk)

G. We _____ already _____ the apartment. (rent)

H. They _____ never _____ there. (work)

I. You _____ enough TV for today. (watch)

J. I _____ just _____ you. (tell)

K. He _____ always _____ here. (live)

L. She _____ finally _____ for it. (pay)

M. We _____ a very nice neighborhood. (find)

N. They _____ already _____ for work. (leave)

The negative of the present perfect tense

I have not seen it. or I haven't seen it.
You have not used it. or You haven't used it.
It has not happened yet. or It hasn't happened yet.
He has not been here. or He hasn't been here.
We have not met before. or We haven't met before.
They have not thought about it. or They haven't thought about it.

PRACTICE USING THE NEGATIVE OF THE PRESENT PERFECT TENSE.
Answer these questions.
Start each answer with <u>No</u>.

A. Have you found an apartment yet?

         No, I haven't found one.

B. Has she called the doctor already?

_____

C. Have they told the landlord about it?

_____

D. Has he heard about the job?

_____

E. Have we reached Main Street already?

_____

F. Have I spelled your name right?

_____

G. Has the airplane left yet?

_____

H. Have you ever traveled to the Far East?

_____

I. Has the doctor examined you?

_____

J. Have we missed the bus?

_____

K. Have I done this right?

_____

L. Has the store closed?

_____

Using there is, there are, is there, are there, and their negative forms

SINGULAR	PLURAL

SINGULAR

Is there a dishwasher?
Yes, there is a dishwasher.
Yes, there's a dishwasher.
No, there isn't a dishwasher.
No, there's no dishwasher.

PLURAL

Are there any bugs?
Yes, there are some.

No, there aren't any bugs.
No, there are no bugs.

FILL IN THE MISSING WORDS.
Use is there or are there to ask a question.
Answer each question.
First answer yes, then answer no.

A. _____Are there_____ two closets in the bedroom? __Yes, there are.   No, there aren't.__

B. _____ any children in the building? _____

C. _____ a laundry room here? _____

D. _____ a train station nearby? _____

E. _____ any screens for the windows? _____

F. _____ a garage in the basement? _____

G. _____ an elementary school in the neighborhood? _____

H. _____ any stores within walking distance? _____

I. _____ two bathrooms? _____

J. _____ a new lock on the door? _____

Asking and answering questions

These are questions words: who, what, when, where, why, how, and which.
Notice how they are used in these questions.
Notice the answer to each question.

QUESTION	ANSWER

QUESTION

Who gave you that book?
What did you eat for lunch?
When did you move to this building?
Where is the nearest bus stop?
Why do you want a new apartment?
How do you get to work in the morning?
Which dress should I buy?

ANSWER

My friend Ralph gave it to me.
I had a tuna fish sandwich.
I moved here two years ago.
It's on the next corner.
Because my apartment's too small.
I take the train.
Buy the red one.

122

PRACTICE USING QUESTION WORDS.
Fill in the question word.
Use <u>who</u>, <u>where</u>, <u>why</u>, <u>when</u>, <u>what</u>, <u>how</u>, or <u>which</u>.
Then answer each question.

A. _____ is your birthday?

_____

B. _____ do you spell your last name?

_____

C. _____ are you learning in English class?

_____

D. _____ were you born?

_____

E. _____ do people need to work?

_____

F. _____ kind of building do you live in?

_____

G. _____ many rooms are there in your home?

_____

H. _____ do landlords ask for a security deposit?

_____

I. _____ is a lease?

_____

J. _____ do you look for sales?

_____

K. _____ supermarket has the best prices in your neighborhood?

_____

L. _____ is it important to lock your door?

_____

Using if

If you don't damage the apartment, you'll get your security
deposit back.
I'll bring a friend along, if it's all right with you.
If you don't hurry, you'll miss the bus.

PRACTICE USING IF.
Answer the questions.
Use if in the answers.

A. You go to English classes. What will you learn?

If you go to English classes, you'll learn to speak English.

B. You eat too much at the restaurant. How will you feel?

_____

C. You go to sleep very late. What will you be like in the morning?

_____

D. You don't pay your electric bill. What will the electric
company do?

_____

E. You forget to take out the garbage. How will your apartment smell?

_____

F. You fall on the ice and break your leg. Where will you have to go?

_____

G. You come to work late every day. What will your boss do?

_____

H. A landlord wants to rent an apartment. What will he do?

_____

I. You use coupons at the supermarket. What will you save?

_____

J. A sales clerk gives me the wrong change. What will I say?

_____

K. I have no heat in my apartment.   What will I do?

_____

L. Tom wants to find a new job.   Where will he look?

_____

PRACTICE ON YOUR OWN

A. Look at newspaper ads for apartments.   Write out the words
for the abbreviations.

B. Find out about some neighborhoods near you.   Ask friends
questions about the shopping, schools, noise, parks, and
transportation.

C. Call about some of the apartments that are for rent.
Ask questions about the rent, lease, security deposit,
pets, children, transportation, etc.

D. Visit some apartments that are for rent.   Visit them even
if you are not ready to rent one.   Find out about the
neighborhood and the building.

E. Get copies of some leases.   Ask someone to help you understand the
leases.   What do they mean?

UNIT 5

IS THERE A GUARANTEE?

IN THIS UNIT YOU WILL LEARN:

how to show that you agree
    (and disagree) with someone
how to show that you are not sure
how to talk about home furnishings
how to describe furniture
how to get a good buy when you are
    shopping
how to understand guarantees and
    warranties
what to say when you want to return
    something to a store

Notice how these words and phrases
    are used in the unit:

**I'm not sure, I guess so, I think,
    perhaps, maybe, I wonder
I'll (let me) think it over
that's true, you're right, that's
    a good idea, I think so, too
I agree, I know**

In this unit you will review these tenses:

simple present, simple past, present
progressive, present perfect,
future with **will**, future with **going to,**
and the negative and question forms of
these tenses

126

LOOK AT THE PICTURE.
Find these words in the picture.

1. television
2. air conditioner
3. microwave oven
4. toaster oven
5. portable radio
6. food processor
7. speakers
8. turntable
9. clock radio
10. electric (space) heater

TALK TOPICS

LOOK AT THE PICTURES.
Talk about what you see.

What is this place?
What can you buy here?
Why were there people sitting on
    the furniture?
Why are some people measuring the
    furniture and appliances?
What do the signs mean?

What are floor samples?
What are easy payment plans?
Which of these appliances do you have
    at home?
Which of the appliances would you
    like to buy?
Have you bought furniture or
    appliances recently?
Where did you buy them?
Talk about your experiences in
    shopping for furniture and appliances.

What are some differences between this
    picture and the first one?
Talk about what has changed.

ASK ABOUT OTHER THINGS IN THE PICTURE.
Use these question words: who, what, where, which, how.
Write your new words.

11. _____   16. _____
12. _____   17. _____
13. _____   18. _____
14. _____   19. _____
15. _____   20. _____

LISTEN TO THESE PEOPLE.
They are talking about home furnishings.

How's your new apartment?

It's OK, I guess. It's pretty empty, though.

Don't you have any furniture?

Not much. I have a bed, a dresser, a table, and two chairs.

You're right. That's not much. Don't you have a sofa?

No. I looked at some in the department store, but they were all too expensive.

I know. Department stores often have expensive furniture. But you can get furniture for a lot less.

How?

Well, you can wait for a sale, or you can go to a discount store, or you can buy used furniture.

What's a discount store?

It's a store that has cheaper prices. But you have to be careful. Always compare prices before you buy.

Why?

Because sometimes they charge a lot more in one store for something than they charge in another.

How can I find the names of different furniture stores?

One way is to look in the yellow pages. Another way is to look in the newspapers for advertisements of furniture sales.

Thanks for the advice.

130

THE YELLOW PAGES

LOOK AT THIS PAGE FROM THE YELLOW PAGES.
You are looking for furniture stores.
Answer the questions.

Furniture Dlrs.-Retail (Cont'd)

LAZY BOY SHOWCASE SHOPPES
THE LARGEST DISPLAY &
BIGGEST INVENTORY
OF LA-Z-BOY RECLINERS IN
THE NASSAU AREA
OPEN SUNDAY 12 TO 5
DAILY INCLUDING SAT. 11 TO 6
MON. - THURS. - FRI. TO 9
CLOSED WED.
334-7177 | 373 Old Country Rd. - Carle Place
Between Fortunoff & Levitz

Lazy Boy Showcase Shoppes
373 Old Country Rd Crl Pl--------- 334-7177

**LIFE STYLES CUSTOM DESIGN
SPECIALISTS IN FURNITURE & WALL
SYSTEMS**
240 Long Beach Rd Isl Pk-------- 432-4454

Little Neck Mirror Ltd
Modern & Conventional Mirrored
Furniture
253-28 Northern Blvd Lt Nk---- 212 224-1541

LOWE FURN INC
Authorized Sealy Posturepedic Dealer
2755 Merik Rd Blmr------------ **826-6000**

LYONS FURNITURE CO
337 Main Hntgtn-------------- **427-0003**

Main St Furniture & Aplnce Corp
10 Main Hmpstd-------------- 489-1866

MAPLE CENTER FURNITURE
3200 Long Beach Rd Ocnsid------ **678-5400**

Mattress Stop Inc
525 Jericho Trnpk Mineola--------- 248-4644

Mercury Office Furniture Inc
51 Bloomingdale Rd Hksvl-------- 938-3155

Mr. Moneybags Cut-Rate Bedding Inc
1339 Hempstd Trnpk Elmnt------- 488-7177

MODERAMA FURN INC

MODERN & CONTEMPORARY INTERIORS
SEE OUR MANY EXCLUSIVE IMPORTS

88-12 Qns Blvd Elm--------- 212 898-3482

NEW DEAL TABLE CORP
Mfrs. Of Wood & Chrome Dinettes
Discount Dining Room, Living Room, Bed
Room Sets, Convertible Sofas, Bedding
6202 16 Av Bklyn----------- 212 259-7195

Perman Bros Inc 283 Frmt Hmpsta---- 481-7421

PORCH & PATIO INC
See Our Display Ad Page 561
315 Sunrse Hwy Rkvl Cntr-------- **764-8100**

Prima Casa Ltd 508 Central Av Cdrhrst- 295-1552

Recliner City 5560 Sunrise Hwy Maspqa 795-5035

Redisch S & Sons Inc
See Our Display Ad Page 559
27 E Bway Manh----------- 212 962-0700

Regal Furniture & Aplncs Co Div Of Royal
Svce Co Of Mineola New York
119 S Main Freprt------------- 546-1435

**RIGHTWAY MATTRESS & FURNITURE
FACTORY OUTLET**
Factory Direct To You One Of Long
Islands Largest Manufacturers
4410 Austin Blvd Isl Pk--------- **431-0847**

ROMA FURNITURE CO INC
Fine Furniture At Low Prices
150 Sunrise Hwy Rkvl Cntr------- **766-0910**
150 Sunrise Hwy Rkvl Cntr------- 766-0911

ROWE FURNITURE—
CONSUMERS FURNITURE PLAN CORP
45 E 20 Manh----------- 212 473-1865

Roxy Dinettes
See Our Display Ad Page 561
770 Hempstd Trnpk Frnkln Sq----- 489-5311

S & S Uneeda Furniture & Sleep Shop
984 Hempstd Trnpk Frnkln Sq----- 437-3030

SACHS NEW YORK
Offices-Phone & Mail Orders
351 Park Av S Manh--Mineola TelNo-**742-1600**
250 Fulton Av Hmpstd---------- 485-7700

SCANDINAVIA LTD FROM
Quality European Craftsmanship
30 Jericho Trnpk Wstbry--------- 997-6777

Schlaefer G Colonial Annex
20 Main Pt Wash-------------- 883-3834

SEAMAN'S FURNITURE CO INC
235 Old Country Rd Crl Pl------- **742-8020**

**SEVENTEEN SEVENTY-SIX CRAFTERS
LTD THE**
**COUNTRY COLONIAL &
EARLY AMERICAN
FURNITURE**
Unique Lamps & Accessories
INTERIOR DECORATING SVCE.
CUSTOM PIECES AVAILABLE
2421 Jericho Tpk Garden City Pk--- 747-8055

SPENCER FURN
Price Us Before You Buy
50 Rkwy Av Vly Strm----------- **825-8855**

**STACEY HOUSE FURNITURE DIV OF
DETROIT FURNITURE**
1200 Broadhollow Rd Frmgdl----- 752-1500
275 W Merrick Rd Vly Strm------- 825-0800

**SUBURBAN COLONIAL FURNITURE
WAREHOUSE OUTLET**
615 Sunrise Hwy Blu Pt--------- **363-2323**

Suburban Furn Corp
See Our Display Ad Page 562
243 Main Hntgtn-------------- 427-1045

SUPERIOR WOODWORKING CO
Ladderbacks - Brentwood - Captain's
Chairs - Unfinished
147 Willis Av Mineola-------------- 746-0211

TABLE FAIR—
TABLES & CHAIRS
● PARSONS FOR ALL NEEDS
● OCCASIONAL & COCKTAIL TABLES
IN STANDARD & ORIGINAL DESIGNS
● CUSTOM MICA BEDS & FURNITURE
● ART FOR HOME
42 Lincoln Pl. | **593-4333**
Lynbrook |
(1 Blk. S. Of Sunrse Hwy. & Atlantic Ave.)

Tiffany Glass & Mirror Ltd
Modern & Conventional Mirrored Furniture
69 Cuttermill Rd Grt Nk--------- 482-1160

A. You are looking for a mattress. A friend told you that Rightway has the best prices. What number will you call? _____

B. Practice with another student. One person recommends a furniture store. The other person finds the name in the listing and gives the phone number.

C. You live in Brooklyn (abbreviated Bklyn). Find the furniture store in the listings above that is located in Brooklyn. _____

D. Some of the stores specialize in a certain kind of furniture. What does Seventeen Seventy-Six Crafters specialize in? Lazy Boy Showcase Shoppes? Mr. Moneybags? Roxy? Tiffany?

E. Practice these same activities with your own local yellow pages.

131

LOOK AT THIS FURNITURE.
Write the names of the furniture pieces under each picture.
Use the words from the furniture list.

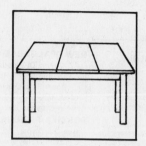

_____

_____

_____

_____

_____

_____

_____

_____

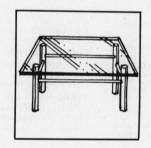

_____

_____

_____

_____

FURNITURE LIST

desk	carpet	dresser
dining table	bed	lamp
sofa/couch	coffee table	night table
armchair	chair	bookcase

LOOK AT THESE ROOM NAMES.
LOOK AT THE LIST OF HOME FURNISHINGS.
Put each thing into a room.
You can put some of the items in any of the three rooms.

KITCHEN

_____

_____

_____

_____

_____

_____

_____

BEDROOM

_____

_____

_____

_____

_____

_____

_____

LIVING ROOM

_____

_____

_____

_____

_____

_____

_____

LIST OF HOME FURNISHINGS

toaster	bookcases	tablecloth	stove
armchair	night table	stereo	pictures
bed	television	clock radio	sofa
drinking glasses	dining table	dresser	mirror
sheets	lamps	draperies	plates
refrigerator	carpet	pots and pans	chairs
chest of drawers	bedspread	pillows	coffee table

TRY IT ON YOUR OWN.
Make a list of the home furnishings you have in one of the
rooms in your house.

_____   _____

_____   _____

_____   _____

_____   _____

133

LISTEN TO THESE PEOPLE.
The sales clerk is trying to get a customer to buy a sofa.
The customer is not sure.

May I help you?

Yes. I'm looking for a sofa.

What style did you have in mind?

I'm not sure.

How much do you want to spend?

About $400 or $500. I saw some on sale.

There aren't too many left.

I thought the sale lasted for a month.

The ad said, "While quantities last."
When these sofas are sold, the sale is over.

I see. But I'm not ready to buy.
I'm just comparing prices.

These sofas are a very good buy.
Would you like to try them?

I guess so. This one doesn't seem
very comfortable. Perhaps another
one would be better.

How about this one?

Maybe it's a little better than the
other one. I'm not sure if I really
like it, though.

This one is only $385, reduced from $600.
It's the last one left in this style.

I guess it's pretty comfortable. I
wonder if it will look good in my
living room?

These colors go with almost anything.

Do you think so? Well, let me think
it over.

FILL IN THE MISSING WORDS.
Practice using words that show you aren't sure.

CLERK: May I _____ you?

YOU: Yes. I'm _____ for a rug.

CLERK: What did you have in _____ ?

YOU: I'm not _____ .

CLERK: How _____ do you want to _____ ?

YOU: Oh, _____ $250. I read an ad that said you have

some on _____ .

CLERK: Do you want to see the _____ on sale?

YOU: I _____ so.

CLERK: There are only a few _____ . Do you _____ this one?

YOU: It's all right, I guess. _____ another one would be nicer.

CLERK: How _____ this one? It's the _____ one left in this

color.

YOU: I _____ if it will look good in my living room.

CLERK: This color _____ with almost anything.

YOU: Well, let me _____ it _____ .

TALK TO THIS SALES CLERK.
You are not sure about which lamp to buy.
The sales clerk wants to sell you one.

SALES CLERK: May I help you?

YOU: _____

SALES CLERK: What style are you interested in?

YOU: _____

SALES CLERK: How much do you want to spend?

YOU: _____

SALES CLERK: These lamps are a very good buy.

YOU: _____

LOOK AT THESE ADS.
Answer the questions.

①

TOP QUALITY CLASSIC
AT GIVEAWAY
PRICE!!

CHAIR & OTTOMAN
IN GENUINE LEATHER

$399⁰⁰

Take advantage
of this outstanding
offer while
it lasts

Small additional charge if delivery wanted

Contempo
FURNITURE CENTER

OPEN SUNDAY 12 to 5

Manhasset   1406 Johnson Blvd   (516) 620-5990
Southampton   24 Main St   (516) 787-8787

②

The sumptuous luxury of
genuine leather

Imagine settling into the
sumptuous luxury of butter soft
leather. Here is the classic chair, a
masterpiece of fine craftsmanship
that swivels and tilts for maximum
comfort. Choice of black, dark
brown, or caramel leather, each
handsomely accented with molded
deep-grained hardwood and
rich chromium. Matching
ottoman included. An
outstanding value at
just $399.

View It Now in
Our Beautiful alpha
Showroom.

alpha
INTERIORS
INTERNATIONAL
916 Third Avenue
New York, NY 10022

List Price
$675.00

alpha Introductory Price

ONLY **$399**

Mon. thru Sat. 9 to 5 – Tel. 549-8363

③

LEATHER
DESIGNS

THE STATESMAN.
GLOVE LEATHER.
50 COLORS. ONLY AT
LEATHER DESIGNS.

Swivel, tilts. Rosewood $420.
Ottoman $155.
Walnut $405.
Ottoman $145.

Catalog of Contemporary Chairs. Leather swatches $1.

146 E. 51st St., N.Y. 10022   (212) 728-1844
Branch: 166 State Hwy., Chambers, N.Y.   (212) 922-1420

Since 1945
35 Years of
Craftsmanship in
Leather Furniture

A. Which chair is the most expensive? _____

B. Which stores don't charge extra for the ottoman? _____

C. Which store has the biggest selection of colors? _____

D. Which ad tells you about a delivery charge? _____

E. Which store gives you a choice of wood? _____

F. What kinds of wood are available? _____

G. Do you think the three chairs are the same? _____

How can you find out? _____

136

READ THESE SHOPPING TIPS.
Answer the questions.

HOW TO BE A BETTER BUYER

PRICE—Ask if the selling price includes delivery, installation, and service charges. These extra charges may add to the cost. Also ask about returns and refunds.

ESTIMATES AND RECEIPTS—On major purchases, get estimates from more than one company. Get receipts for all payments, as well as for appliances taken from your home or left for repair.

SERVICE AND REPAIR—Check the cost of service calls by telephone. Ask the repairman for an estimate of the total cost of repair, then get an itemized bill before paying.

CONTRACTS AND CREDIT DETAILS—Don't be rushed into signing a contract if you are unfamiliar or unsure. Ask for a copy to take home for a careful review. Learn the terms, interest rate, and payment plan. Be sure to keep a copy of everything you sign.

GUARANTEES—All guarantees and promises should be in writing. Find out who is responsible for carrying out the terms of the guarantee. If there is a registration card, be sure to send it in.

PROBLEMS—If you run into problems, call your local Better Business Bureau, Department of Consumer Affairs, or Consumer Protection Board.

Adapted from the MANHATTAN CONSUMER YELLOW PAGES, © 1981 New York Telephone Co.
Reprinted with the permission of the copyright owner.

A. Read the tip about PRICE. What three extra charges can add to the price of an item?

_____

B. What should you do before you buy something big (a major purchase)?

_____

C. What should you ask about when you call for service or repair?

_____

D. What should you do with a contract before you sign it?

_____

E. A salesman tells you the store guarantees everything they sell. But he will not give you a written guarantee. Is the guarantee valid?

_____

F. Who can you call if you have problems with a company?

_____

I'm looking for a dining table.

Did you have a certain kind in mind?

No. I'm not sure what I want.

Well, we have round, oval, square, and rectangular tables.

I think I'd like a round one.

Here's a nice modern round table. It has a glass top.

Oh, it's nice, but I don't think I want glass.

How about this one, then? It's made of oak.

Oak? It's beautiful. Perhaps it's too small, though.

It comes with two leaves.

Leaves?

Yes. They're inserts. You pull the table apart like this and put a leaf in. Now the table is larger.

I think I'd like a lighter wood. How about this square one? What kind of wood is it?

It's not wood. It's a plastic that looks like wood.

Is it cheaper than wood?

Yes, and it doesn't scratch or stain as easily.

I don't know. May I just look around?

Certainly. Let me know if I can help you.

DESCRIBING FURNITURE

LOOK AT THESE WORDS.
They are used to describe furniture.
Add other words.

MATERIALS	SHAPES	DIMENSIONS	STYLES
wood (oak, maple, etc.)	round	height (high)	modern
glass	square	length (long)	contemporary
leather	rectangular	width (wide)	colonial
plastic	oval	depth (deep)	Spanish
vinyl	_____	across	French provincial
velvet	_____	twin-size	Mediterranean
brass	_____	full-size	Oriental
chrome		queen-size	_____
_____		king-size	
_____		_____	
		_____	

TALK TO THIS PERSON.
Practice describing furniture.
Tell a sales clerk what you are looking for.
Use words from the lists and other words you know.

A. I'm looking for a rectangular chrome-and-glass cocktail table.

B. (a sofa) _____

_____

C. (a bookcase) _____

_____

D. (an armchair) _____

_____

E. (a bed) _____

_____

F. (a dresser) _____

_____

USED FURNITURE

LISTEN TO THESE PEOPLE.
They are talking about buying used furniture.

Hi, Rick. What's new?

I'm fixing up my new apartment.

Oh. What have you bought?

Nothing yet. I've looked for a sofa, but I can't find a cheap one.

Have you looked at the sales in the department stores?

Yes, but they're still too expensive.

How about the discount stores?

The same. If I spend all my money on a sofa, I won't be able to buy the other things I need.

Have you looked for a used sofa?

Where?

Look in the newspaper. People put ads in the paper when they want to sell things.

Used sofas?

Yes. Maybe they're moving or redecorating. It's worth a try. You don't have to buy anything you don't like.

That's true. But if I find something, how will I get it home?

I have a friend who has a van. I'm sure he'll let me borrow it. I'll help you. Call me when you find something.

That's very nice of you.

What are friends for? I'll speak to you soon.

LOOK AT THESE ADS.
They are for used home furnishings.
Answer the questions.

A.

Lv. Rm. Set - 8 Pcs. - $600. King sized
Bedrm set w/large mirror $600 - 997-7819.

1. What size is the bed?

_____

2. What does "8 Pcs." mean?

_____

B.

COLONIAL Couch, chair ottoman & Conv.
Queen sofa. TV 9″ portable, b/w, Spears
a/c, all excellent. 669-0075.

1. What style is the couch?

_____

2. What does "b/w" mean?

_____

C.

MAHOGANY Table, 2 rugs: 6′x4′ Bokahara;
9′x12′ Oriental. 4 oriental lamps. 5 piece
bdrm set- Antique white, 2 pr. drapes. Ken-
mort sewing mach. w/cabinet & chair.
481-3353.

1. What comes with the sewing
   machine?

_____

2. What kind of wood is the table
   made of?

_____

D.

CONTEMPORARY wall unit includes book
shelves; record storage; bar; magazine
rack; 4 free-standing components total 120″
in length. Perfect cond., $500/best offer.
333-8985 Eves.

1. How big is the wall unit?

_____

2. What does "$500/best offer" mean?

_____

E.

LARGE RUST RECLINER. Like new, $150.
Will deliver if necessary. Call 671-0092
before 10 a.m. or weekends.

1. What does "rust" mean in this ad?

_____

2. What will the seller do if necessary?

_____

TRY IT IN CLASS.
Practice with another student.
One student is the seller. The other is the caller.
The caller asks about the furniture in the ad.
The seller describes the furniture.

DINING ROOM Set, 6 low-back chairs,
breakfast server, excellent condition, Asking
$1,275. BEDROOM, complete set, modern,
'Natural Mahogany'. Asking $950. Call 997-
7909.

141

LISTEN TO THESE PEOPLE.
They are shopping for a new TV.
They agree with each other.

There are so many TVs. It's hard to choose.

I know. It's very hard to decide.

Isn't this one like your brother's?

You're right. It's just like his.

I think his TV works really well.

Yes, it does.

I wonder how much he paid for it. This one seems very expensive.

It is a lot of money. Why don't we buy a smaller one of the same brand?

That's a good idea. This one is too big for our living room anyway.

Here's a smaller one. The picture is perfect. Is there a guarantee?

Let's see. Here's the warranty. It's guaranteed against defective material and workmanship for two years.

What does that mean?

If something goes wrong with it, the company will fix or replace it—unless we damage it, of course.

How does the company know when you bought it?

Here's a warranty registration card. We have to send it in, and we have to save the receipt.

Well, this one looks good. What do you think?

I think so, too. Let's get it.

TALK TO THIS PERSON.
Practice showing that you agree.
Use phrases like: you're right; I agree; I know; I think so, too;
that's true; that's a good idea.

PERSON: I really think we need new chairs for the kitchen.

YOU: _____

PERSON: Aren't these chairs like the one in the restaurant?

YOU: _____

PERSON: Well, if they use them in a restaurant they must wear well.

YOU: _____

PERSON: I think they're pretty comfortable. How about you?

YOU: _____

PERSON: They're not very expensive, are they?

YOU: _____

PERSON: I think we should get them. What do you think?

YOU: _____

TRY IT IN CLASS.
Practice with another person.
Tell the person that you agree or disagree.
If you disagree, use phrases like: I don't agree, I don't think so,
I don't like that idea.

PERSON: People in the United States use too many appliances.

YOU: _____

PERSON: Charge accounts make people spend more than they can afford.

YOU: _____

PERSON: You should never buy on credit. Save up for what you want.

YOU: _____

PERSON: It's better to shop in a small store than in a department store.

YOU: _____

A WARRANTY

LOOK AT THIS WARRANTY.
It is a written guarantee for an appliance.
Read it in class.

WARRANTY

This appliance is guaranteed against defective material or workmanship for one full year from the date of purchase. During the warranty period this product will be replaced or repaired at no charge to the owner if there is evidence of defective workmanship or parts. This guarantee does not cover damage due to abuse, mishandling, unauthorized repair, or commercial use. In the event of a defect, please deliver the product to the nearest authorized service station listed on the reverse of this warranty (or look in your local yellow pages for your nearest authorized service station). The Use and Care Booklet included with this appliance will direct you in its proper use.

FILL IN THE WARRANTY REGISTRATION CARD.
Fill in the informaton about a Fresco Coffeemaker,
Model Number PK 01B, Serial Number 1071, purchased on
August 4, 1982.

WARRANTY REGISTRATION CARD

Fill out the information below and return this card to the manufacturer named on the reverse within two weeks of the purchase of the appliance.

Owner's Name _____

Address _____

City _____ State _____ Zip _____

Serial Number of Product _____

Model Number _____

Date of Purchase _____

Name of Store _____

TALK TOPICS.
Talk about the warranty and warranty registration card.
Answer the questions.   Discuss your answers.

A. How long is the appliance guaranteed for?

   (1)   for one year after you start using the appliance
   (2)   for one year after you buy the appliance
   (3)   for one year after the appliance is made

B. What is the "warranty period"?

   (1)   the time it takes to fix the appliance
   (2)   the time you have to send in the registration card
   (3)   one year from the time you bought the appliance

C. What is "defective material or workmanship"?

   (1)   a mistake in how the appliance is made or put together
   (2)   a mistake the owner makes when he uses the appliance
   (3)   a mistake made by an unauthorized repair person

D. Which of the following damages is not covered by the guarantee?

   (1)   an appliance that falls apart because it was not glued properly
   (2)   an appliance that has a part missing from it
   (3)   an appliance that was dropped by the owner

E. Which of the following damages is covered by the warranty?

   (1)   a coffee pot that breaks after it is used in a
         restaurant for three months
   (2)   a coffee pot that stops working after the owner leaves
         it plugged in for two days
   (3)   a coffee pot that falls apart after it is used at home
         for three months

F. What should the owner do with the appliance if it doesn't work well?

   (1)   take it back to the store where he bought it
   (2)   take it to one of the manufacturer's service stations
   (3)   mail it back to the factory where it was made

G. When should the owner send in the registration card?

   (1)   a year after buying the appliance
   (2)   when the appliance is damaged
   (3)   within two weeks after buying the appliance

LISTEN TO THESE PEOPLE.
They are talking about returning something to a store.

Can I help you?

Yes. I'd like to return this toaster.

Is there something wrong with it?

No. I decided to buy another kind.

Do you have your receipt?

Yes, I do. Here it is.

OK. Let me check the box. It seems all right. Would you like credit or a refund?

I'd like my money back, please.

OK. I'll fill out a refund slip. You'll have to go to customer service for your refund.

I want to return this radio.

Do you have your receipt?

No, I got it as a present.

Are you sure it was bought here?

Yes. Here's a ticket with the store name on it.

OK. But I won't be able to give you a refund. I can only give you credit.

Credit? I don't understand.

I'll write out a credit slip. Then you can buy something else in the store with it.

What if I don't find something I want?

You can save the credit and use it another time.

OK. Thanks.

TALK TOPICS

A. What is a receipt?

B. Why should you save receipts?

C. Why do people return things?

TALK TO THESE PEOPLE.
Practice returning something to a store.

A. You are returning a stereo. You saw another one you
liked better. You have your receipt and the original box.

YOU: _____

SALES CLERK: Is there anything wrong with it?

YOU: _____

SALES CLERK: Do you have your receipt?

YOU: _____

SALES CLERK: Would you like credit or a refund?

YOU: _____

B. You are returning a blender. You got it as a present.
You don't have a receipt. You would like a cash refund,
but the clerk tells you that you can only have credit.

YOU: _____

SALES CLERK: May I have your receipt?

YOU: _____

SALES CLERK: I'll have to give you a credit slip, then.
Please fill out your name and address on it.

YOU: _____

SALES CLERK: I'm sorry. We don't give cash refunds without
a receipt.

YOU: _____

C. You bought a vacuum cleaner and took it home. You
noticed that some of the parts were missing. Tell
the sales clerk. Ask for another one. Check the
box of the new one to make sure all the parts are there.

YOU: _____

SALES CLERK: I'm sorry that you had a problem. May I see your receipt?

YOU: _____

SALES CLERK: I'll bring you another one right away.

YOU: _____

SALES CLERK: Here it is. This one should be all right.

YOU: _____

SALES CLERK: Certainly. I'll open the box for you.

YOU: _____

TRY IT IN CLASS.
Practice with another student.
One of you is a customer. The other is a sales clerk.

A. The customer is returning an appliance. The sales clerk asks
about the receipt and gives a refund.

CUSTOMER: _____ (want to return)

SALES CLERK: _____ (receipt?)

CUSTOMER: _____ (yes)

SALES CLERK: _____ (refund or credit?)

CUSTOMER: _____ (refund)

SALES CLERK: _____ (at customer service)

B. The customer is returning a vacuum cleaner. He doesn't
have a receipt. The sales clerk can only give store credit.

CUSTOMER: _____ (want to return)

SALES CLERK: _____ (receipt?)

CUSTOMER: _____ (no)

SALES CLERK: _____ (store credit)

CUSTOMER: _____ (OK)

148

CLOSE-UP ON LANGUAGE

Review of the tenses

Simple present:	She <u>buys</u> all her clothes on sale.
Present progressive:	She <u>is buying</u> a new sweater right now.
Simple past:	She <u>bought her</u> coat at Spear's last year.
Present perfect:	She <u>has bought</u> five dresses already.
Future with <u>will</u>:	She <u>will buy</u> another one next week.
Future with <u>going to</u>:	She's <u>going to buy</u> one tomorrow.

Close-up on the present tense

FILL IN THE MISSING WORDS.
Use the present tense.

A. I _____ work _____ in a tall building.   (work)

B. You _____ a good job.   (have)

C. She _____ to work at 8:30.   (go)

D. He _____ late again.   (be)

E. We _____ in an English class.   (be)

F. You _____ at the door.   (pay)

G. They _____ to each other on the phone.   (talk)

H. He _____ a wife and a child.   (have)

I. I _____ very hungry.   (be)

J. She _____ all of the work.   (do)

Close-up on the present progressive tense

FILL IN THE MISSING WORDS.
Use the present progressive tense.

A. They _____ are looking _____ for a new apartment.   (look)

B. We _____ late again.   (work)

C. He _____ in an armchair.   (sit)

D. She _____ to the sales clerk.   (talk)

E. I _____ prices.   (compare)

F. The sales clerk _____ a new radio for you.   (get)

G. They _____ lunch right now.   (have)

H. The children _____ across the street.   (run)

I. We _____ a party for her.   (give)

J. He _____ a letter to his mother.   (write)

Close-up on the past tense

FILL IN THE MISSING WORDS.
Use the past tense.

A. I ____bought____ this bed on sale.   (buy)

B. He _____ very happy to see you.   (be)

C. She _____ three slices of pizza.   (eat)

D. We _____ $5.00 for each ticket.   (pay)

E. They _____ at the movies last night.   (meet)

F. My mother _____ dinner for ten people.   (make)

G. My friends _____ a very good time.   (have)

H. You _____ me your name, but I forgot it.   (tell)

I. I _____ your coat by mistake.   (take)

J. They _____ us their old dresser.   (give)

Close-up on the present perfect tense

FILL IN THE MISSING WORDS.
Use the present perfect tense.

A. I see that you _____have met_____ each other already.   (meet)

B. They _____ at all the chairs in the store.   (look)

C. We _____ this train many times.   (take)

D. You _____ her once before.   (see)

E. He _____ the chair he wants to buy.   (find)

F. She _____ all that she can do.   (do)

G. I _____ it over.   (think)

H. We _____ with her for three years. (live)

I. The kids _____ their dessert already. (have)

J. My sister _____ me all of her old furniture. (give)

Close-up on the future with <u>will</u>

FILL IN THE MISSING WORDS.
Use the future tense with the word <u>will</u>.

A. I ____will ask____ my friend for the van. (ask)

B. They _____ here soon. (be)

C. We _____ for you at the station in the morning. (look)

D. You _____ money at a discount store. (save)

E. He _____ you if he needs you. (call)

F. You _____ better after a nap. (feel)

G. I _____ you where the escalators are. (show)

H. She _____ late on Sunday. (sleep)

I. They _____ you extra for delivery. (charge)

J. You _____ exact change for the bus. (need)

Close-up on the future with <u>going to</u>

FILL IN THE MISSING WORDS.
Use the future tense with <u>going to</u>.

A. We ____are going to make____ a shopping list before we go. (make)

B. You _____ a good time, I'm sure. (have)

C. He _____ a lot for a new color TV. (pay)

D. She _____ the apartment for the new tenant. (paint)

E. I _____ a sofa when I have enough money. (buy)

F. They _____ at newspaper ads for used furniture. (look)

G. The store _____ a sale next month. (run)

H. I _____ prices before I buy. (compare)

I. You _____ help moving the furniture. (need)

J. We _____ this on our charge account. (put)

READ THESE SENTENCES.
Change the tense of each verb and write a new sentence.
What does the new sentence mean?
Talk about it in class.

A. We <u>will wait</u> for you at the exit at 5 o'clock.

Yesterday, _____ we waited for you at the exit at 5 o'clock _____ .

B. They <u>are going to buy</u> a new table for $400.00.

Last year, _____ .

C. She <u>is talking</u> to the sales clerk.

_____ many times.

D. He <u>tried</u> on a gray suit.

_____ right now.

E. We <u>live</u> in the city.

_____ for five years.

F. I <u>returned</u> the toaster to the store.

_____ tomorrow.

G. I <u>have looked</u> at all the chairs.

_____ before I buy one.

H. I'll <u>find</u> out about it on Friday.

_____ last Friday.

I. She <u>works</u> in the supermarket.

_____ since September.

J. He <u>thought</u> it over.

_____ and let you know.

LOOK AT THE WORDS.
Use them to write a sentence.
Change the verb to the correct tense. Put the words in order.

A. We/wait/for/minutes/twenty   (past tense)

_____ We waited for twenty minutes. _____

B. They/pay/check/by   (present progressive)

_____

C. I/for/look/armchair/an   (present progressive)

_____

D. She/buy/yesterday/new/a/of/pair/shoes   (past)

_____

E. You/try/already/size/this/on/   (present perfect)

_____

Question forms

Simple present:	<u>Do you live</u> in an apartment?
Present progressive:	<u>Are you living</u> there now?
Simple past:	<u>Did you live</u> there last year?
Present perfect:	<u>Have you lived</u> there a long time?
Future with <u>will</u>:	<u>Will you live</u> there for another year?
Future with <u>going to</u>:	<u>Are you going to live</u> there next year?

PRACTICE USING THE QUESTION FORM.
Change these sentences into questions.

A. We are going to meet you at the exit after work.

      Are we going to meet you at the exit after work?

B. She has worked late every night this week.

_____

C. We opened a charge account at the department store.

_____

D. They'll return the smaller coffee pot.

_____

E. This sweater fits me perfectly.

_____

F. You have used all of your coupons.

_____

G. I gave her the right change.

_____

H. He is going to lend me the van.

_____

I. The store will stay open late tonight.

_____

J. I am walking toward the river.

_____

Negative forms

Simple present:	We don't pay much rent.
Present progressive:	We are not paying (aren't paying) that much for a movie.
Simple past:	We didn't pay for the desk yet.
Present perfect:	We have not paid (haven't paid) the bill yet.
Future with will:	We will not pay (won't pay) for her dinner.
Future with going to:	We are not going (aren't going) to pay for it.

PRACTICE USING THE NEGATIVE FORM.
Change these sentences into the negative.

A. We are going to think it over.

_____ We are not going to think it over. _____

B. They have looked at everything.

_____

C. I saw that movie last week.

_____

D. You look very nice in that suit.

_____

E. She will be very happy when she sees this.

_____

F. The window opens easily.

_____

G. The landlord is giving too much heat.

_____

H. They are going to move in on the first.

_____

I. I talked to her last night.

_____

J. We have told you everything we know.

_____

PRACTICE ON YOUR OWN

A. Look in your local yellow pages. Find the page that lists
the furniture stores.
Write down some of the words you don't understand.
Ask someone to explain them to you.

B. Visit some furniture stores that are near your house.
Pick out a piece of furniture, like a sofa or wall unit,
that you want. Talk to the sales clerks. Ask them
about the furniture.

C. Find out about the quality of appliances. Get a copy
of a consumers' guide or consumers' handbook at a library.
Ask a friend to help you find out about an appliance you want.
Find out which of the brands is the best.

D. Go to some department stores and discount appliance stores and
compare the prices of the appliance you want. Ask about
delivery and installation costs. Ask about guarantees.

E. Find out about buying on credit. What does it mean to buy on
credit? Ask a friend or a sales clerk about it.

F. Find out how you can qualify for credit from a department store.
Talk to someone in customer service.

G. Find out how much an appliance will cost if you pay it off
little by little. Ask a sales clerk.

H. Is it better to save up for an appliance or a piece of furniture
or to buy it on credit and pay for it little by little? Talk
this over with some friends and relatives.